3

CULTURES OF THE WORLD

INDONESIA

Gouri Mirpuri

MARSHALL CAVENDISH
New York • London • Sydney

Editorial Director	Shirley Hew
Managing Editors	Mark Dartford
	Shova Loh
Editors	Goh Sui Noi
	Meena Mylvaganam
	Cheryl M. English
Picture Editor	Jane Duff
Production	Jeremy Chan
	Robert Paulley
	Julie Cairns
Design	Tuck Loong
	Doris Nga
	Stella Liu
	Lee Woon Hong
Illustrators	Thomas Koh
	Francis Oak
	Vincent Chew

Reference edition published 1990 by
Marshall Cavendish Corporation
147 West Merrick Road
Freeport, Long Island
N.Y. 11520

Printed in Singapore by
Kim Hup Lee Printing Co. Pte Ltd

Originated and designed by
Times Books International
an imprint of Times Editions Pte Ltd
Times Center, 1 New Industrial Road
Singapore 1953
Telex: 37908 EDTIME Fax: 2854871

Library of Congress Cataloging-in-Publication Data:
Mirpuri,Gouri, 1960–
      Indonesia /Gouri Mirpuri—Reference ed.
        p. cm.—(Cultures of the world)
      Includes bibliographical references.
      Summary: Introduces the geography,
history, government, commerce, people and culture
of Indonesia.
      ISBN 1-85435-294-6: $19.95
      1. Indonesia—Juvenile literature.
[1. Indonesia.] I. Title.
DS615.M54 1990
959.8—dc20
                89-25457
                CIP
                AC

INTRODUCTION

SOME PEOPLE imagine Indonesia as it was a century ago, when ships returned from these Spice Islands laden with exotic spices and priceless treasures. For some it is impenetrable rain forests, for others, the tourist-brochure beaches of Bali.

In reality Indonesia is such a kaleidoscope of landscapes and lifestyles that it is hard to imagine any country with a similar degree of diversity, from the violent volcanoes to the peaceful padi terraces, from the dreaded headhunters to the cultured Javanese. Today, this oil-rich nation is a newly developing country, all geared up for take-off into the new century.

This book attempts to go beyond simple stereotypes of Indonesians to help us better understand the nation and its people. It is part of the series, *Cultures of the World*—a look at people and their lifestyles around the world.

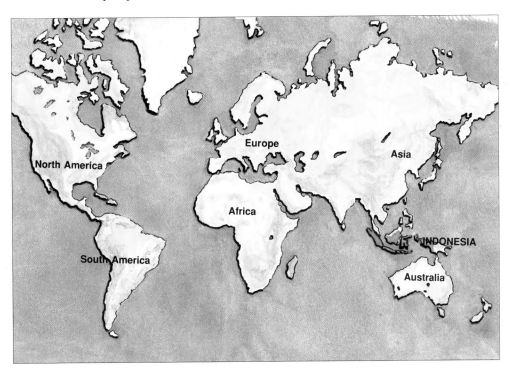

CONTENTS

Girls in costume on the island of Java.

Moslems in prayer, the women on the right, the men on the left.

CONTENTS

East Timorese women in traditional costume.

GEOGRAPHY

LARGEST ARCHIPELAGO IN THE WORLD

INDONESIA, the largest archipelago in the world, lies between 6° North and 11° South at the crossroads of the continents of Asia and Australia/Oceania. This strategic position has greatly influenced its cultural, social, political and economic life.

Indonesia stretches 3,977 miles between the Indian and Pacific Oceans, which is the width of the United States of America, or the distance from Oregon to Bermuda. If the water space between the 13,700 scattered islands is included, Indonesia covers 1.9 million square miles, or 2½ times the size of Australia! As 80% of the area is in fact water, Indonesians refer to their country as *Tanah Air Kita*, which literally means "Our (Nation of) Land and Water."

Indonesia's five main islands are Sumatra (slightly larger than California), Java (almost the size of New York State), Kalimantan, on the world's third largest island, Borneo, Sulawesi (about the size of Great Britain), and Irian Jaya, part of the world's second largest island, New Guinea. The other islands, of which only 6,000 are inhabited, vary in size from rocky outcrops to larger islands.

Opposite: **Besides luxurious rainforests such as this, one can also find monsoon and montane forests with chestnuts, laurels and oaks, alpine meadows and mangrove swamps on the Indonesian archipelago.**

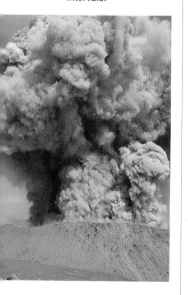

GEOLOGICAL HISTORY

The Indonesian islands were formed during the Miocene period about 15 million years ago, seemingly a long, long time ago but only yesterday on the geological time scale. The islands were created along the line of impact between the shifting Australian and Pacific tectonic plates. The Australian plate is slowly drifting upwards into the path of the Pacific plate, which is moving south, and between these fault lines lie the Indonesian islands.

This makes Indonesia one of the most volatile geographical regions in the world. The mountainous spine, which runs right through the archipelago, contains more than 400 volcanoes, 70 of which are active. Wherever you go in Indonesia, you are unlikely to lose sight of the characteristic huge conical shape, smoke billowing from its top. Forming part of the Pacific "Ring of Fire," Indonesia experiences about three tremors and earthquakes a day and at least one volcanic eruption a year.

The ash and debris regularly spewed out by the volcanoes are washed down and deposited in the alluvial plains. This ash is Indonesia's life-sustaining material. The whitish deposit is so rich in chemicals that it has resulted in some of the most fertile soils in the world: push a stick in the ground and it will soon sprout leaves! Three rice crops can be produced a year without the use of fertilizers, providing the staple food for a country ranking among the most populated in the world.

THE BIG BANG

On August 27, 1883, the infamous volcano Krakatoa erupted in one of the biggest and most cataclysmic explosions in history. The eruption ripped a huge chunk of the earth's crust forming a gaping 16-square-mile hole under the sea. As the peak of the volcano collapsed into this hole, the sea rushed in and produced a catastrophic tidal wave.

Imagine an explosion so tremendous that:
- It blew the island it was on to pieces.
- It produced the loudest sound on earth, which was heard in Colombo and Brisbane 2,500 miles away.
- It caused a tidal wave 98 feet high which swept across the coast of Java killing 35,000 people.
- It rocked the boats in the English Channel.
- It flung 7,000 cubic feet of rocks and debris 17 miles into the sky.
- The debris landed on Madagascar, across the Indian Ocean, and caused spectacular sunsets all over the world for the next three years.
- The ash reached Singapore, 522 miles away.
- Everything was pitch black for two days in the Sunda Straits.
- The atmospheric waves produced by the eruption circled the globe seven times.

Today, in its place, is *Anak Krakatoa*, "Child of Krakatoa." Seismologists constantly monitor this young volcano for threatening signs or indications of a repeat performance, while geologists and biologists study the life-forms which have evolved on the island.

Continental drift and more recent tectonic plate movements have also divided Indonesia into three natural areas with widely differing flora and fauna. The Wallace Line, named after the naturalist who first made the observation, demarcates these three regions: the Sunda Shelf, the Sahul Shelf and the Lesser Sundas.

The broad, shallow Sunda Shelf is actually an extension of mainland Southeast Asia. The islands of Java, Sumatra and Kalimantan are located here. During the last Ice Age, when sea levels dropped, these islands were probably not only connected to each other but also to the Asian mainland.

Map of Indonesia showing how the Wallace Line divides the archipelago into three distinct regions of flora and fauna.

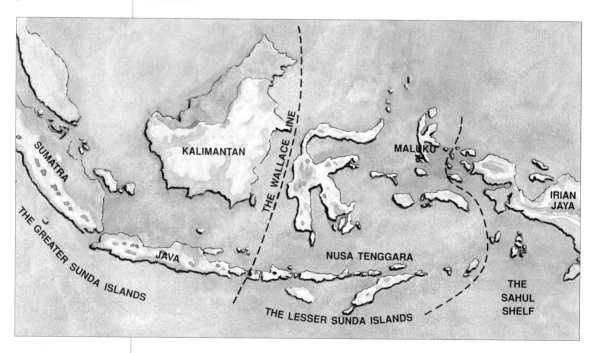

Left and below: **The three regions demarcated by the Wallace Line have very different flora and fauna. For example, the one-horned rhinoceros of Java (left) is similar to animals of the Asian mainland as the Sunda Shelf was once connected to it. The vegetation of Maluku (below) is typical of the Lesser Sunda region. Animals one associates more with Australia, such as tree kangaroos and wallabies, are found in Irian Jaya which is on the Sahul Shelf.**

On the east is another broad expanse, the Sahul Shelf, which contains the island of Irian Jaya. This island, half of which is New Guinea, was probably torn off from Australia during a rift movement. In fact, if we look at a map of the region, New Guinea fits exactly into Northern Australia, like two pieces of a jigsaw puzzle.

Between these two shallow shelves is the Lesser Sunda region. It includes the islands of Sulawesi (previously called Celebes), Maluku and Nusa Tenggara.

CLIMATE

Since Indonesia straddles the equator, it experiences the typical year-long hot and humid pattern of tropical countries. With humidity levels often rising to 100%, most days tend to be sticky.

Indonesia has only two seasons, and even these are not extremes. The "dry season" lasts from June to September, while the "wet season" is from December to March. During the dry season, the islands come under the influence of winds from the southeast which originate in Australia. The wet season brings rain from northeasterly winds, moisture-laden after traveling over the South China Sea.

Rain is perhaps a mild word to use in this region. During the monsoons, such tremendous walls of water explode from the sky that it is like standing under a huge waterfall! Actually, most of Indonesia experiences at least some rain throughout the year, a characteristic of being in the equatorial "ever wet" zone.

Temperatures do not vary a lot, but are lower in the mountains. Being surrounded by the cooling sea lowers the temperature to a tolerable 80°F along the coastal plains, but you are likely to get a bad sunburn if you are out in the mid-day sun. As you go higher, the temperature drops by 2°F every 656 feet, resulting in a very pleasant 68° to 72°F in the highlands. Many Indonesians frequently escape to the mountains to spend their vacations "cooling off" from the heat of the lowlands. As the temperature falls with altitude, you also end up with anomalies like the famous Mandala Mountains in Irian Jaya which are snow-capped in spite of being right on the equator!

The Antarctic landscape of the Mandala Mountains in Irian Jaya. This is one of four summits with eternal snow, mist and high winds in this tropical country.

FLORA

Most of Indonesia is covered in evergreen equatorial rainforests, with those in Kalimantan dating back 35 million years. However, one is just as likely to find mangrove swamps with their looping aerial roots in Eastern Sumatra and large tracts of arid savannah grassland in the Lesser Sunda Islands. At higher altitudes, there are alpine meadows containing chestnuts, laurels and oaks more reminiscent of Switzerland than a tropical country.

The abundant rainfall and high humidity has produced some of the densest forest in the world. The trees form a thick canopy preventing the sun from penetrating the lower levels where numerous parasitic plants strain upwards in search of light. These forests are also self-fertilizing as the plants decompose to form rich humus very quickly after they die.

THE LARGEST FLOWER IN THE WORLD

Found only in the jungles of South Central Sumatra, the immense *Rafflesia arnoldi* leads a parasitic existence at the base of certain trees. The plant has no leaves but its bud bursts open every couple of months to reveal five huge dark red petals with white specks. This is the world's largest bloom, which can measure more than 3 feet wide and weigh up to 20 pounds.

Indonesian flora is not only abundant but also exotic and incredibly diverse, with over 40,000 species recorded to date. The trees form such a mosaic that it is unlikely you will find areas of one type of tree anywhere.

There are valuable trees like teak, ebony, sandalwood, camphor, clove and nutmeg; brilliant orchids ranging from the 10-foot-long Tiger Orchid, the largest in the world, to the tiny *Taeniophyllum* which is edible and used in medical preparations; exotic plants such as the carnivorous pitcher plant, which traps insects in its liquid-filled cups and extracts their nutrients; strange parasitic creepers including the Strangler Fig which grows aerial roots to eventually strangle the very tree on which it grows; and monstrous flowers such as the *Rafflesia* (see box).

One species of plant found in the equatorial rainforests is the parasitic *Rafflesia*.

15

FAUNA

The British naturalist Alfred Wallace made one of the most significant discoveries about this region while exploring the East Indies in the 1850's in a tiny sailing vessel. Wallace was struck by the existence of a clear boundary beyond which the animals typical of India and Malaysia had hardly spread. Climate could not have been a deciding factor as it was similar throughout, so there had to be another explanation.

The explanation was found in the last Ice Age, when the water level dropped so low the islands on the shallow Sunda Shelf were connected to the Asian mainland. Today you can find similar tropical animals inhabiting both these regions. This also explains why the animals found in Irian Jaya, located on the now submerged Sahul Shelf, are similar to those found in Australia. In between, the Lesser Sunda Islands were in an area too deep to link up with any land mass and remained isolated. These islands contain many endemic species, animals which are unique to this region alone.

Indonesia boasts an incredible variety of birds, insects, lizards, snakes, fish and other animals: the one-horned rhinoceros of Java; the Orang Utan (literally "Man of the Jungle") with its blazing orange shaggy coat found only in Sumatra and Kalimantan; 14-inch-high miniature deer; the Atlas moth with a wing-span of 10 inches; the brilliantly plumaged Bird of Paradise which is unable to fly; the enormous hornbill; the Komodo Dragon (see box); and others. The list is long and fascinating. Irian Jaya alone is world-famous for its birds, and so far, more than 670 species have been recorded. A concern for preserving this wildlife has led to several nature reserves being set up throughout Indonesia.

Various conservation programs have been initiated to halt the extinction of the Orang Utan, one of the many rare animals found in Indonesia.

THE LARGEST LIZARD IN THE WORLD

Although dinosaurs are extinct, their latter-day relatives, the fierce Komodo Dragons, have survived for millions of years in Indonesia, particularly on the island of Komodo. These huge lizards can measure up to 10 feet long and weigh 300 pounds. They have immense, scaly bodies supported on short, muscular legs and massive, lethal tails. Their razor-sharp teeth are used to rip apart their daily feed of goat, deer and wild pig.

Historians believe the famous Chinese dragon was fashioned after this creature, whose long, forked, blazing orange tongue resembles fire.

Although several hundred dragons are found in Indonesia, barely a dozen are surviving in zoos outside the country: in captivity, they usually become fat and then die.

The world's only *real* dragons are the Komodo Dragons.

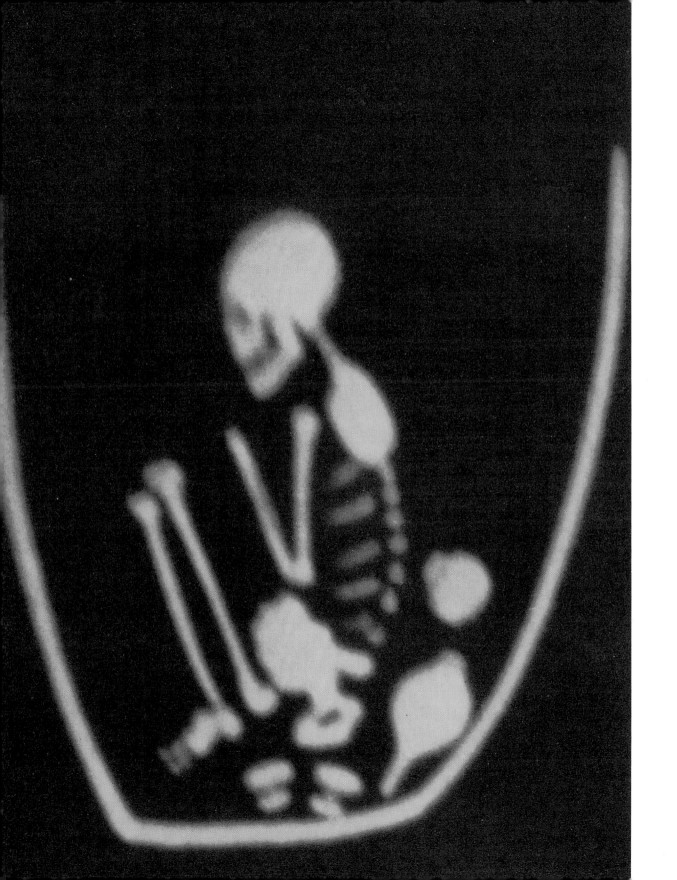

HISTORY

PREHISTORY

THE FIRST MODERN MAN in Indonesia was undoubtedly the dark-skinned, wooly-haired, pygmy Negrito who belonged to the Australoid group. He was the first *Homo sapiens* to come to Indonesia, about 30,000 to 40,000 years ago. Nobody knows where he came from exactly, but his genetic traces can still be found in Eastern Indonesia, as in the highland tribes of Irian Jaya.

The Negritos were followed several centuries later by people of the Australoid group. They were also dark-skinned and wooly-haired, but had broad, flat noses and pronounced brow ridges. It is not clear whether they originated in Africa or India, but today many tribes which reside in the remotest islands and jungles of Indonesia bear a striking resemblance to them.

Both these groups were soon driven into the highlands and jungles by Mongolian migration from the north. There seems to have been two major movements out of the overpopulated northern Indochina region: that of the Proto-Malays and that of the Deutro-Malays.

The Proto-Malays, represented today by ethnic groups such as the Bataks and Dayaks, brought with them a Neolithic, or New Stone Age, technology. They lived in village settlements, domesticated animals and cultivated food. Evidence of their culture can be seen today in the huge stone monuments, or megaliths, found in Sumatra.

The Deutro-Malays belonged to the true Mongoloid race. How they came to Indonesia is still a mystery, but they soon took over the best agricultural lands, driving the other inhabitants into the highlands and jungles. Today, their descendants are found along the coasts and plains of all the major islands, and constitute the majority among Indonesia's ethnically diverse population.

Opposite: **An X-ray photograph of a two thousand-year-old jar, which was once used as a burial urn, found in West Java.**

THE HINDU-BUDDHIST KINGDOMS

Prambanan, completed sometime around A.D. 856, is considered by many to be the finest monument in Java.

In the 2nd century A.D., India was at the peak of its cultural development. The Indonesian ruling class, impressed with India's philosophical, religious and cultural superiority, started to "Indianize" their own kingdoms. They invited Brahmin scholars to their courts; sent students to study in India; learned about astronomy and navigational techniques, figure sculpturing and textile dyeing; borrowed numerous Sanskrit words which are still in use; introduced spices such as cardamom and turmeric into their food; domesticated horses and elephants; and changed their architectural style.

However, the two biggest areas of change were in the new social status of the rulers and in religion. The Indonesian aristocracy found they could better control their kingdoms once they introduced the Indian concept of a divine ruler—perhaps a descendant of some mythical figure or a reincarnation of the Hindu god Vishnu himself—with limitless powers and belonging to the highest "caste."

India's twin religions—Hinduism and Buddhism—began a peaceful coexistence in Java and Sumatra. Later, the Hindu god Shiva and Lord Buddha were treated as reincarnations of the same God, thus further blurring the distinction between the two religions.

By about the 8th century there were two well-established kingdoms: the Buddhist Srivijaya kingdom in Sumatra which ruled the seas and major marine routes for the next 600 years, and the Hindu-Buddhist Mataram and Sailendra kingdoms of Central Java which controlled inland rice production for a shorter period of time. In fact, Sumatra was called Swarnan Dwipa, or "Gold Island," while Java was called Java Dwipa, or "Rice Island."

The Srivijaya kingdom was based on foreign trade, and controlled the strategic Straits of Malacca. From here, spices, incense and other rare goods were traded between China and India.

The Javanese Mataram and Sailendra kingdoms were more culturally oriented. The rich soils and wet-rice agriculture supported a huge population, much of which was later employed for the building of the magnificent Borobudur (see page 22) and Prambanan temples. This peaceful coexistence of Hindus and Buddhists did not last long; after a turbulent 300 years or so, there emerged a powerful new Hindu kingdom in Java called the Majapahit. Established in 1294 in an area known for its *pahit* (bitter) maja fruit, this empire marked the Golden Age of Indonesian history. It was then that a true Indonesian identity emerged and a unique Javanese art and culture developed and flourished.

However, around the 14th century this great kingdom went into decline and was soon invaded by the new Islamic state of Demak. The entire Hindu-Javanese aristocracy fled to Bali, leaving behind a rich heritage which even until today shows how close the Indian-Indonesian bond was.

If you ever get the chance, "see Borobudur during the full moon or in the very early morning when layers of mist fill the valley and . . . conical volcanoes shine in the morning sun" (Dalton, *Indonesia Handbook*). Approach the gentle pyramid from the west and walk clockwise through its ten terraces to pay tribute to the gods. It is three miles to the top.

BOROBUDUR

Rising high above the rolling rice plains of Central Java is ancient Borobudur, the largest Buddhist monument in the world. Built sometime between A.D. 778 and A.D. 850 by the Sailendra princes, it took almost a century for more than 10,000 peasant laborers, carvers and sculptors using basic hand tools to complete the colossal structure.

Borobudur was buried under volcanic ash and tropical growth for centuries until in 1814, the British Governor of Java, Sir Stamford Raffles, attempted uncovering what was rumored to be a "mountain of Buddhist sculptures in stone." Unfortunately, Borobudur was plundered by the Dutch for the next 100 years. Sections of carved panels and Buddha heads were removed for use as decorations in the gardens of the rich or as gifts to visiting dignitaries.

International criticism halted the plunder, and the Dutch made another unsuccessful attempt at restoring the monument: every time it rained, the soft base would wash out until finally the structure was in danger of collapse.

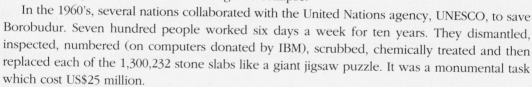

In the 1960's, several nations collaborated with the United Nations agency, UNESCO, to save Borobudur. Seven hundred people worked six days a week for ten years. They dismantled, inspected, numbered (on computers donated by IBM), scrubbed, chemically treated and then replaced each of the 1,300,232 stone slabs like a giant jigsaw puzzle. It was a monumental task which cost US$25 million.

The relief and carvings along the narrow corridors and galleries represent stages in a person's life as he aims for perfection. The lower square terraces (the square symbolizes earth) show passion and desire. The next levels depict tales from the Buddha's life and at the three circular terraces right on top (the circle symbolizes heaven), we enter the world of formlessness and perfection. At this level there are 72 stupas with perfectly carved life-size Buddhas sitting inside. For good luck, one should reach through the stone lattice to touch the sacred statues within.

THE COMING OF ISLAM

When Marco Polo visited Indonesia in 1292, he noted that Islam was already established in parts of Aceh in north Sumatra. The religion had come there through Arab traders plying the India-China trade route.

From Aceh, Islam spread to the rest of Indonesia. The religion went from east to west along the trade routes and the paths of economic expansion. To help spread the religion, rulers placed the royal *gamelan* orchestras in meeting halls which were hurriedly turned into mosques. People from the surrounding areas came to listen and were converted. By the 15th and 16th centuries many Indonesian rulers had made Islam the state religion, persuaded by the desire to strengthen ties with Malacca, which had then become the center of Islam and of trade. This allowed them to enter the growing international Islamic trade network which brought yet more power and wealth. Islam was also a more egalitarian religion than Hinduism, professing the "equality of all men before God," which had great appeal to the common people.

In the 16th century the Islamic kingdom of Demak attacked the weakening Hindu Mataram kingdom in Central Java, taking control of its rich lands and driving the Hindu elite east to Bali. The fall of this once-great empire was recorded by Moslem court chroniclers as "the disappearance of the light of the Universe."

Above: **Conservation work on Borobudur continues in laboratories to help maintain this magnificent monument.**

Opposite: **A statue of the meditating Buddha atop Borobudur.**

THE EUROPEANS

Jan Pieterszoon Coen, an accountant by profession, founded Batavia in 1619. His motto was *Dispereet niet!* ("Do not lose hope.")

Attracted by the spices of the Indies, the Portuguese too found their way to the spice islands of Maluku. Their profits encouraged other European traders to come to this region and, while the English explored the Malayan peninsula and the Spanish the Philippines, the Dutch arrived in Indonesia.

In 1596, 4 Dutch ships arrived at Banten after a difficult 14-month voyage during which more than half of the 249 crew members had died. The remaining sailors were unruly and created a negative impression in Java, but the few spices with which they returned home caused so much excitement that, over the next 10 years, 65 more Dutch ships came to Indonesia looking for trade.

Soon, by means more foul than fair, the Dutch established a foothold in Jayakarta (modern Jakarta), which they renamed "Batavia." They started sinking the ships of any other country found in Indonesian waters, forcibly took over the spice islands of Banda and, after more bitter, bloody fighting, controlled clove-producing Sulawesi.

Left: **A 19th century Dutch painting of early Batavia by P. Lanters.**

Below: **A slave market in old Batavia. The slaves were worked hard and cruelly punished.**

By the end of the 17th century they controlled not only the spices, but also monopolized the production of coffee, sugar, indigo, pepper, tea and cotton on several islands. The powerful Dutch East India Company (VOC in Dutch initials) was established to manage this trade and the resulting huge profits.

The entire island of Java was now being run as a forced-labor camp, much like the 19th century slave plantations of the southern United States. However, this domination was achieved at great military expense, and the constant resistance that the Dutch army experienced finally proved too costly. By 1799, the VOC went bankrupt in what was perhaps the largest commercial collapse in history.

THE SEEDS OF RESISTANCE

The Dutch did little to educate the masses. Ninety percent of the local population was not educated at all. By the 1920's a handful of colleges were opened and some Indonesians were sent to Holland for education. When these scholars returned, they had also learned about Dutch rule and oppression, and began agitating for freedom.

Two of the national heroes who emerged during this period were Diponegoro and Kartini. In the early 19th century, Diponegoro, a very popular Javanese prince, fought a guerrilla battle against the Dutch for 5 years which cost 200,000 Javanese and 8,000 European lives, mostly through starvation and cholera. Tricking him with the bait of a negotiation, the Dutch eventually arrested and exiled him, thus crushing the resistance.

Raden Kartini was a less fiery but equally admired hero. Tired of being a pampered princess, she expressed her frustrations at the denial of higher education to Indonesians. In the 1910's, she wrote a series of powerful yet sensitive letters to a Dutch couple in Holland, which, when published, caused a stir among the foreign community.

Meanwhile, back in Indonesia, the first National Party (the PNI) was formed under the leadership of a former engineer named Soekarno. Soekarno was a gifted speaker and charismatic leader. He became so powerful that he was soon arrested and exiled with other leaders. By then, however, the concept of an Indonesian nation had been proclaimed in the famous Youth Pledge of 1928: "One People, One Language, One Nation."

Raden Ajeng Kartini (1879–1904), Indonesia's first woman liberator and one of the country's most-honored national heroes.

THE JAPANESE

Independence still seemed a long way off. When the Japanese arrived during the Second World War, the Indonesians, thinking it signified liberation from Dutch oppression, welcomed them with open arms. The Japanese *did* throw out the Dutch, but immediately began an even more ruthless exploitation of the Indies. The reports of the three-and-a-half year Japanese occupation chronicle numerous atrocities, from the use of mass slave labor in the jungles of Burma and Malaya to the starvation which resulted when the entire rice crop of Java was exported to Japan.

In order to increase their power and spread propaganda, the Japanese promoted the Indonesian language, Bahasa Indonesia, as the national language. They also attempted to unite the scattered islands by supporting the nationalists. Both these moves backfired however: the confidence they gave the people prompted the nationalist leaders, Soekarno and Hatta, to declare Indonesia's independence on August 17, 1945, just one week after the second atomic bomb destroyed Nagasaki.

After the end of the war, the Dutch tried to take advantage of the situation to regain control of Indonesia. International condemnation coupled with Indonesian nationalistic efforts forced the Dutch out.

Finally, after centuries of struggle under oppression, the people could truly declare a free and independent Indonesia.

Schoolchildren welcoming the invading Japanese forces. Most Indonesians thought the Japanese would liberate them from Dutch rule. A 12th century king of Java had prophesized that the arrival of "yellow men" from the north would free Java from the rule of "despotic white men."

Right: **Monumen Lubang Buaya**, the memorial for the army officers brutally executed and thrown into a crocodile hole ("*lubang buaya*"). Thousands were killed in the anarchy that followed. Today this period is remembered as the darkest in Indonesia's history.

Below: Soekarno, Indonesia's first President, reading the Proclamation of Independence on August 17, 1945.

INDEPENDENT INDONESIA

The years following independence were not easy, with over 169 parties struggling for power. In 1959, Soekarno declared martial law and established his policy of "Guided Democracy," initiating a period of intense nationalism and anti-colonialism during which the West was blamed for all of Indonesia's woes. Things came to a head by 1965, dubbed "The Year of Living Dangerously." On the night of September 30, members of the Communist Party and a group of young army radicals kidnaped, tortured and brutally killed six leading generals and an officer. Conflicting reports describe what happened that eventful day, but within a few hours General Soeharto moved in to crush the coup.

The next twelve months saw hundreds of thousands of communists killed and thousands more imprisoned. Students demonstrated on the streets demanding the banning of the Communist Party, lower prices for food and other essentials and a change of Soekarno's cabinet. Finally, on March 11, 1966, the once all-powerful Soekarno was persuaded to sign a document which would stop the riots and hand the presidency over to General Soeharto.

With political peace came economic prosperity. Upon his appointment, Soeharto quickly imposed martial law and banned the Communist Party. He also broke ties with communist China and the U.S.S.R. and revised Indonesia's foreign policy, re-entering the UN as its 60th member.

Within Indonesia the entire civil service was reorganized. The economy slowly stabilized, setting out a path of high growth through sensible policies aimed at increasing foreign investments, boosting oil export, decreasing population growth and increasing food production. Soeharto's economic "New Order" had begun.

GOVERNMENT

THE NATIONAL LEVEL

THE HIGHEST POLITICAL INSTITUTION is the MPR or the People's Consultative Congress. It has 1,000 members from a cross-section of society—farmers, workers, students, businessmen—who meet every five years to decide on state policy, sanction the constitution and elect a president.

The DPR, or House of Representatives, is just below the MPR. It is made up of 500 members, all of whom also belong to the MPR. These 500 people are elected to the DPR every five years and consist of members from each of the three main socio-political organizations: the ruling GOLKAR (Joint Secretariat of Functional Groups), the PPP (the United Development Party) and the PDI (the Indonesian Democratic Party). In addition, 100 members from the armed forces are appointed to the DPR. Aside from its traditional military role, the Indonesian armed forces also takes on a socio-political role and thus is often described as *dwi-fungsi* or having a "dual-function."

The President is both Indonesia's Head of State and its Chief Executive. He is elected to a five-year term but may be re-elected indefinitely. The President appoints a Cabinet of Ministers to carry out state policy, and is ultimately responsible to the MPR for all decisions.

Opposite: **The MPR or Indonesian Parliament in session.**

The lines of power and responsibility within the legislature.

```
        THE MPR (The People's Consultative Congress)
        ┌──────────────────────────┬──────────────────┐
  THE PRESIDENT                          THE DPR
                                  (The House of Representatives)
  THE CABINET

  THE MINISTERS
```

THE REGIONAL LEVEL

Indonesia is divided into 27 provinces, including the three special territories of Jakarta, Yogyakarta and Aceh. Each province has a capital and is headed by a governor. The provinces are further divided into districts, each with a *bupati* (regent) as its head. Within the districts are hundreds of little towns and villages, headed respectively by the *walikota* (mayor) and village heads. Just as the President is guided by and responsible to the MPR, the village head is guided by the village council of elders.

The hierarchy of power.

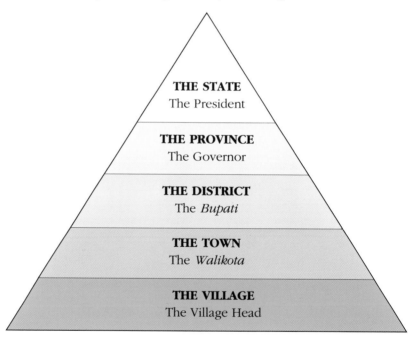

THE STATE
The President

THE PROVINCE
The Governor

THE DISTRICT
The *Bupati*

THE TOWN
The *Walikota*

THE VILLAGE
The Village Head

HOW DECISIONS ARE MADE

Whether at the top-most level of state or down in the tiny villages, all Indonesians make decisions in a similar manner. This is through *Musyawarah* (consultation) and *Mufakat* (discussion) until a consensus is reached. It is a very long and tiring process.

In Indonesian-style democracy, everyone's views are heard and considered and taken into account towards developing a consensus solution acceptable to all.

This goes hand in hand with the concept of *Gotong Royong*, where everyone works together rather than in competition, to achieve common goals. Whether it is a flood, volcanic eruption or just the *padi* (rice) which needs to be cut, everyone in the village comes with their own tools and volunteers to help a needy neighbor. In this way, anyone in trouble gets help, and the job gets done much faster.

Villagers harvesting a rice field together in *Gotong Royong* (mutual assistance).

PANCASILA DEMOCRACY

Like the United States, Indonesia follows a democratic presidential system of government. And as the U.S. has its *Bill of Rights* and England its *Magna Carta*, Indonesia has its *Pancasila*, or "Five Principles." The democracy practiced is based on these five principles, and is called *Pancasila* Democracy. These principles, declared by President Soekarno in 1945, are a combination of ideas with a focus on traditional village customs.

Pancasila now serves as a way of life for Indonesia's millions, who learn about it in school, when they work for the government and throughout their lives. In fact, the entire first week of the new school term is called "*Pancasila* Week."

Each of the five *sila,* or principles, of *Pancasila,* the state policy, is represented on the Coat of Arms.

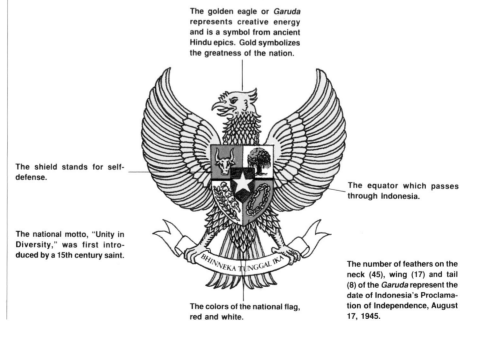

The golden eagle or *Garuda* represents creative energy and is a symbol from ancient Hindu epics. Gold symbolizes the greatness of the nation.

The shield stands for self-defense.

The equator which passes through Indonesia.

The national motto, "Unity in Diversity," was first introduced by a 15th century saint.

BHINNEKA TUNGGAL IKA

The number of feathers on the neck (45), wing (17) and tail (8) of the *Garuda* represent the date of Indonesia's Proclamation of Independence, August 17, 1945.

The colors of the national flag, red and white.

PANCASILA, THE FIVE PRINCIPLES

Today, the values of *Pancasila* constitute the state policy and the life philosophy of all Indonesians.

The star.

1 Belief in One Supreme God
All Indonesians believe in a God and follow one of four great world religions—Islam, Buddhism, Hinduism or Christianity.

The unbroken chain of humanity (the circles represent women, the squares men).

2 Just and Civilized Humanity
Indonesians do not tolerate oppression, physical or spiritual, of any person.

The head of a wild buffalo.

3 Nationalism and the Unity of Indonesia
In 1928, Indonesia's youth pledged to have one country, one nation and one language, binding together the diverse people of the archipelago.

The banyan tree.

4 Indonesian-style Democracy
There is discussion (*Musyawarah*) and mutual assistance (*Gotong Royong*) to reach consensus (*Mufakat*). It is also referred to as *Pancasila*-style democracy.

Sprays of cotton and rice.

5 Social Justice
An equal distribution of welfare and the protection of the weak.

ECONOMY

IN THE ECONOMIC FAST LANE

WHEN PRESIDENT SOEHARTO took over the presidency from Soekarno, the economy was in shambles. Foreign debt was more than US$2 billion and the people were on the verge of starvation.

Swift economic reforms transformed the country. With proper five-yearly plans, foreign investment and astute leadership, Indonesia's development entered the fast lane and is prospering at an incredible speed. In 1970 its Gross Domestic Product was US$11 billion; in 1985 it had increased to almost US$87 billion. The average annual income per person rose from US$80 to US$520. And the country became self-sufficient in rice, its biggest import.

Opposite: **The modern city of Jakarta, capital of Indonesia.**

Map of Indonesia showing the archipelago's crops, natural resources and industries.

Chemicals	Coffee	,Fishing	Natural gas
Coconuts	Corn	Iron	Oil

Palm oil	Rice	Soybeans	Textiles
Pearls	Rubber	Sugar cane	Timber

An oil refinery in Balikpapan. When oil prices fell in 1986, there was a tremendous downturn in the economy. However, with careful management and diversification into other industries, Indonesia was saved the fate which befell other oil-dependent countries.

SOURCES OF REVENUE

MINERALS AND ENERGY Indonesia has always been at the center of an international trade thoroughfare. In the early days it was known as the "Spice Islands." Today the biggest money earner is oil, accounting for more than two-thirds of its export earnings. As a member of OPEC, Indonesia produces a quota of 1.5 million barrels a day, although its potential is estimated at nearly ten times that amount.

Liquefied Natural Gas (LNG) is the second largest earner of foreign exchange for Indonesia, the world's largest exporter of LNG. The gas is sold worldwide to countries such as Japan, South Korea and Taiwan.

Indonesia is extremely rich in tin (it is the world's fourth largest producer), coal, iron sands, copper, bauxite, nickel, gold and silver. Most mining concerns are run by Japanese and Americans.

INDUSTRY This plays a crucial part in Indonesia's diversification aimed at reducing its over-dependence on oil. However, industries employ less than 10% of the population. There is an active light manufacturing sector involved in everything from producing handicrafts to assembling foreign cars. There are also substantial cement, fertilizer, timber processing, steel and oil-related industries. Indonesia's greatest pride is its impressive super-high-technology aerospace industry.

AGRICULTURE Indonesia remains predominantly an agricultural country. More than 60% of the population works on the land, generating about half its non-oil and gas exports.

Indonesia ranks as the world's third largest producer of rice. Much of this has been achieved because the chocolate-colored soils in the inner islands are so enriched with volcanic ash they can yield three rice crops a year. The introduction of high yielding varieties in 1968 has also helped. On these inner islands most of the rice is grown on terraced *sawah* or "wet rice" fields, as has been the case for the last 2,000 years.

On the outer islands where the soils are not as rich and there is less population pressure on the land, *ladang* or "slash and burn" techniques are more popular. This involves clearing several acres of forest land, using it for planting crops for a couple of years, and moving on once the soil is completely depleted. This does not allow the soil to regain its fertility. Environmentalists are concerned that these practices will cause the depletion of hundreds of acres of precious rainforests.

In 1986, when oil prices fell dramatically, there was a frantic call to diversify into non-oil exports. Indonesia is the world's top producer of cloves, the second largest producer of rubber, and the fourth biggest coffee grower. Palm oil, tea and tobacco outputs have also risen appreciably.

Left: **The alluvial soils of the lowlands is the country's life-sustaining material, allowing three rice crops from "wet rice" fields.**

Below: **Environmentalists are concerned by "slash and burn" techniques of farming which deplete the land of nutrients.**

Lake Braten, one of the many tourist attractions on the island of Bali.

TOURISM The government is encouraging the opening up of the outer islands to tourism, especially the isolated eastern islands. Bali is already well known, and the numerous beautiful islands of Indonesia make the country's tourism potential virtually limitless.

FISHING AND FORESTRY Being an archipelago, the potential of the fishing industry is estimated at ten times the present output. Indonesia also has a large forest reserve, second only to the Amazon. Its forestry industry is so active, it has become a major environmental concern.

Some Indonesian children help to supplement the family income by selling food and drinks.

PEOPLE

INDONESIA is the fifth most populated country in the world—after China, India, the Soviet Union and the United States—with its population of 175 million growing at the alarming rate of 2.1% every year.

What is even more startling is the distribution of these people. More than 60% of the entire population lives on Java, an island which accounts for only 7% of the total land area of Indonesia. So with almost 1,000 people crammed into every 0.4 square mile, Java is the world's most densely populated agricultural land. What makes the problem potentially explosive is that at the present rate, Java's population will double in 30 years. In contrast, Kalimantan, which accounts for over 25% of Indonesia, is home to a mere 4% of the population.

Opposite: **Indonesia has a very young population with 42% under the age of 15 and less than 5% over 65.**

Left: **Java is one of the most heavily populated areas in the world. Over 100 million people live on an island the size of England.**

Overcrowding in the major cities has caused slums, much like this one along the Ciliwang River in Jakarta, to develop.

Most Indonesians live in rural areas. In fact, Indonesia is a nation of villages, with a count of 61,341. This does not mean that the cities are empty. On the contrary—like everywhere else in the Third World—the rural poor flock to the big cities in search of jobs, money and excitement. Jakarta, the largest city in Indonesia, doubled its population in the last 20 years; in 1989 a staggering 8 million people lived in this congested metropolis.

Indonesia's population is a young one, with about one-third of the people under 20 years of age. One explanation for this is that since most people are fairly poor they like to have several children in the hope of being supported by them. The life expectancy is also very low, although better medical care is pushing it beyond the present 56 years.

To ease this population pressure, there is a vigorous family planning policy as well as unique "Transmigration Programs" (see box).

TWO IS ENOUGH

Population pressure is a problem only in Java and Bali. In the rural areas, the farmers have tiny 1.5 acre plots to work, and are unable to survive off the land alone. In the urban centers, the situation is worse, as the teeming millions are crammed into tiny shacks in congested slums, along narrow back alleys and beside the railway tracks.

"Two is Enough" is the motto of the active National Family Planning Coordinating Board. The success of the program is seen by the fact that 60% of couples use contraception today. One factor which has helped is that the preference for boys is not as pronounced as in countries such as China and India. Family planning has become such an open topic in Indonesia that in the villages "King and Queen of Contraception" contests are held! And in the cities it is perfectly proper to ask people what contraception method they use, a question which always takes the uninitiated visitor by surprise.

The other way of easing the population pressure has been through transmigration. First introduced by the Dutch in 1904, this involves resettling families from the over-populated "inner" island of Java to the under-populated "outer" islands. Those who decide to transmigrate are the poorest and most desperate families from the urban and rural areas. Once they reach their new homes, they are given five acres of land, a house, one year's supply of food, basic farming tools and seeds to start life afresh.

Critics of this scheme say that the expense of moving and resettling people far outweighs the tiny dent it makes in Java's total population. However, the program has had its successes.

The five *rupiah* coin, the smallest denomination of money, depicts the country's population policy: a couple with two children.

A Balinese family.

ETHNIC HISTORY

The most fascinating aspect of Indonesia is the incredible variety of people who reside here. This is a country with over 100 distinct ethnic groups and 300 languages. This is a land where four of the world's major religions are followed, where prayers are offered to Allah (Islam), God (Christianity), Shiva (Hinduism) and Buddha (Buddhism). The people of Indonesia have such differences in skin and hair coloring, hair type, height and features that it is hard to fathom how they came to be one country.

There are two theories about how such a diverse group of people populated the Indonesian archipelago. The first, the Wave Theory, suggests that large groups of people migrated in waves over several centuries from the Asian mainland.

The other theory is that there was no such well-coordinated mass movement; instead, the various races which came to Indonesia did so in small groups, mixed and mingled with the local people and gradually, over several centuries, replaced the original inhabitants.

What is certain is that there have been influences from at least four

distinct groups of people over the centuries: the Negritos, the Australoids, the Proto-Malays and the Deutro-Malays. Of course, movement then must have been relatively easy because during the last Ice Age the sea level was low enough for the islands of the Sunda Shelf to be linked to mainland Southeast Asia.

Many of the tribes of Irian Jaya live in isolation from the modern world. Here a group are fascinated by a polaroid picture of themselves.

ETHNIC GEOGRAPHY

In this country of scattered islands, high mountains and dense jungle, it is the sea that unites and the land which divides. Thus one is likely to find similarities among people along the coasts of adjoining islands but huge differences between the inner and outer regions of individual islands.

All in all there is an extraordinary differentiation of language and culture across the archipelago, and in a country with over 300 ethnic groups, there are bound to be stereotypes: ". . . all Javanese speak softly and indirectly, all Bataks like to laugh, play the guitar and are aggressive, all Balinese carve and dance . . ." In reality, however, one is just as likely to meet a loud Javanese, a serious Batak or a Balinese who has not held a carving chisel in his entire life. What follows on the next two pages are fact-based attributes of the major ethnic groups in Indonesia.

The caucasian-looking Acehnese are staunch Moslems. They are reputedly fine craftsmen and boat builders. Aceh, in north Sumatra, was a major trading center for centuries and the first place Islam came to in Indonesia.

The Badui are a fascinating people who live in the isolated highlands of West Java where they first fled to escape Islam. Here they live by strict practices of their own and are forbidden from taking any form of transportation or learning writing which is believed to have "secret powers." The white-robed "inner" Badui who live in the heart of the homeland are even more strict, and are believed to have mystic and clairvoyant powers.

The isolated Dayaks, who have a rich tradition of art, live in longhouses along rivers in the jungles of Kalimantan. They use blowpipes for hunting and are animistic, believing in the spirit of things, especially the life-providing river. Head-hunting has only recently stopped, although tattooing and wearing several metal rings to elongate the ear lobes are still seen as signs of beauty.

The Balinese are Hindu and their religion determines much of their lifestyle. The preparations for elaborate temple, cremation and other ceremonies take up most of their energies. Balinese art is world-famous, with each village specializing in a particular creative craft.

The sturdy Bataks live in north-central Sumatra. Many Bataks are Christians, the largest Batak Christian group living around the picturesque Lake Toba district. They are a proud, conservative people. Many are musically inclined and become singers and band leaders.

The Javanese constitute more than half of Indonesia's population. Java has always been the center of Indonesian history because its rich volcanic soils have attracted so much attention. This explains its highly developed culture, art and language. Today, rural Javanese live in overcrowded villages and grow rice on tiny plots.

The Minangkabau are a matrilineal society where the women are the inheritors of the family's wealth and where the men live with the woman's family after marriage. Divorce and remarriage are common, as is migration outside their native region of West Sumatra. There has always been a large Minangkabau representation in politics and government.

The Minahasa are Christians and largely Eurasian, that is, of European and Asian background. As their homeland, Northern Sulawesi, is close to the Philippines, there are cultural links between the two. The Minahasa are well-known for their lavish feasts and large gatherings.

Ever since the 14th century, the Bugis have been the dreaded sea-pirates of the Indonesian waters in their colorful, wind-driven sailboats. They are expert boat makers and have been traders (and pirates) for centuries. They sail without compasses, claiming they can "smell" coral reefs or approaching tidal waves.

The Toradjanese are rugged, mountain-dwelling people famous for the eerie effigies of their dead which guard limestone cliffs in central Sulawesi. They worship the buffalo, wear headdresses of buffalo horns, sacrifice the animal on major occasions and give buffaloes to the bride's family in marriages.

The Sundanese occupy the western third of Java. They are famous for their *wayang golek* (wooden puppets) and the haunting sounds of their hollow flute.

Over a century ago, Chinese men came to Indonesia to work in Dutch plantations and mines. Their wives were only allowed to join them in the early 20th century. Today many of this largest alien group have local names, though the degree of assimilation varies. *Totok* Chinese are first-generation Chinese in Indonesia.

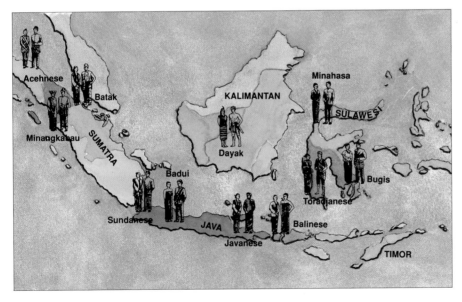

No. of persons (per square mile)

- less than 5
- less than 25
- approximately 45
- approximately 200
- more than 250

LIFESTYLE

ATTITUDES

IN SPITE OF THE superficial identification with western trends such as music, fashion, movies and junk food, Indonesians have their unique lifestyles, ways of looking at and doing things. Given the range of ethnic and religious affiliations and variations, lifestyle is determined by each group's *adat* or "customs." Generally, the typical Indonesian is described as a friendly, somewhat over-polite, happy person who is relaxed in both his attitude toward efficiency and being on time.

THE SOCIAL WEB

Indonesians strive to conform with the group rather than be different. "Doing your own thing," or deviating from the norm, is considered embarrassing and unnatural.

The first allegiance is to one's family. In Indonesia, however, the family extends to grandparents, uncles, aunts, first and even second cousins. In the big cities, anyone from the same village is called *saudara* or "relative." In return, the family provides the greatest support. Relatives can rely on each other—from paying for a child's education or a grandparent's medical bill to emotional support in times of crisis.

After the family comes the obligations of the wider group, for example the clan, village, mosque, neighborhood and work-related organizations.

Opposite: **It is hoped that women will only have two children each in the future. This policy is an attempt to curb the population growth of the fifth most populated country in the world.**

The *sarung kebaya*—the
traditional costume of
Javanese women.

Opposite: **Javanese royal
costumes.**

BEING A GOOD JAVANESE

Many aspects of Javanese culture have become associated with Indonesia
in general as they are the country's largest ethnic group. Centuries of
Hindu influence have refined social behavior so a visitor is quickly struck
by the intricate rules of etiquette and concern with politeness.

The Javanese do not like anything startling or unpredictable to disturb
their single, seamless vision of the world. Their existence is a calm and
peaceful one. Nobody should upset this stability. When something
unpleasant cannot be avoided, however, it is dealt with by maintaining
an outward calm. Many foreigners are taken aback when they see the
tragic news of a dying child or loss of property being told with a smile,
or even a nervous laugh. No one thinks of it as being funny; a smile just
masks the emotional upset.

An Indonesian hates confrontation, preferring to hide negative feelings such as jealousy and anger. He does not complain or shout, but copes with stress by smiling and quietly withdrawing. If egged on beyond this, however, an Indonesian is likely to lose control or even run amok in blind anger, a word that incidentally has its origin in this region.

Even in conversation, a Javanese always strives to "maintain the peace." This often means speaking in a roundabout, indirect manner—to ask for a glass of water, he might clear his throat and comment on how dry and dusty the day is; he never upsets a host by refusing an invitation, even if he knows he cannot make it to the party. It often takes foreigners several months before they understand what is dubbed "Java Talk!"

The Javanese way of life is also manifest in their elaborate rules of etiquette. There is an overriding concern for correct form and politeness, especially when giving respect to elders. People talk in low, even tones with no dramatic arm-flinging or eye-gaping even in times of great excitement. Extreme emotions like uncontrollable laughter or wails of sorrow indicate lack of self-control and inner refinement.

"One has arrived, in Javanese, when one has come to enjoy making the obvious comment at the proper time in the appropriate tone."

—Ward Keeler, in Javanese: A Cultural Approach

A river or stream is very often the "bathroom" for the village.

DIFFERENT FOLKS WITH DIFFERENT STROKES

FLEXIBLE TIME Time is structured very differently in Indonesia. The day begins at sunset, so "last night" is considered earlier the same day. Indonesians have a very laid-back approach to punctuality—a person can arrive between an hour to three hours late without causing offense. When you ask someone the time, it is rounded off to the nearest quarter or even half hour; there is no need to be exact.

BATHING Indonesians bathe at least twice a day, and the more water splashed around, the cleaner and better. In a typical bathroom one does not climb into the stone storage basin or *mandi*. Icy cold water is splashed from this *mandi* over oneself for an invigorating bath which leaves everything soaking wet.

Most rural homes do not have toilets and to defecate one goes to a nearby stream. A squat toilet is usually a hole in the ground with footrests on either side. There is usually no flush system nor toilet paper, as water is preferred for reasons of hygiene.

SICKNESS Medical facilities are used hesitatingly. Most mild illnesses are treated at home and come under the general umbrella of *masuk angin,* literally "the entrance of wind." To protect against this, Indonesians wrap themselves in warm clothes. It is not uncommon to see workers wearing zipped-up black leather jackets under the intense midday sun. To cure any illness due to *masuk angin,* oil is rubbed onto a person's neck and back with a heavy metal coin which is vigorously scraped along the skin. The deep amber stripes which remain for a day or two actually look much worse than they feel.

INTIMACY Public displays of intimacy between people of the opposite sex is not considered proper, though it is perfectly acceptable for friends of the same sex to walk hand in hand. Kissing in public is taboo.

Being treated for *masuk angin* by rubbing a coin along the body.

FORGIVENESS Asking forgiveness for any errors made is a part of the national ethic and the main feature of Javanese politeness. At Lebaran Moslems formally beg forgiveness for wrong-doings of the past year from family and friends. When leaving a job the same is done of one's colleagues and superiors. The apology is always accepted gracefully and everyone starts on a clean slate.

THE SELAMATAN

In Indonesia rites of passage vary depending on ethnic group, status, age (the young prefer to simplify things) and other details such as the money available. What all Indonesians have in common is the indispensable *selamatan*. This communal thanksgiving feast celebrates turning points in an individual's life such as birth, circumcision, death and the start or completion of a major project. It is also an indicator of a person's wealth and status, usually measured by attendance. Every effort is made to ensure this number is large.

The host provides the entertainment: a *gamelan* or *wayang* performance or, more popular now, a tape recorder attached to loud-speakers to produce the festive ambience. Special ceremonial foods are prepared, incense burned and Islamic prayers intoned. In the royal courts even larger *selamatans* are held on religious occasions.

SEMANGAT, THE LIFE FORCE

Many things in nature are believed to contain a vital energy or life force called *semangat.*

In a person, *semangat* is contained in the head, blood, heart, hair and nails. Children are not patted on the head, which is considered sacred, and cut nails and hair are carefully disposed of as these can be used for sorcery. A child's first haircut is a significant event, and tying together a few strands of the bride and groom's hair symbolizes the strength of their union. Head-hunters believed that returning home with enemy heads augmented one's powers, just like the powers of a *keris* (dagger) increased with the number of times it had drawn blood.

There are ritual precautions to appease the spirits contained in important crops such as rice. Clothes, sacred heirlooms and jewelry contain the soul of the previous owner and the *semangat* of mountains, lakes, and old trees must also be handled with due respect.

A chicken is sacrificed in a housewarming ritual to appease the spirits.

Due to the high infant mortality rate, children are guarded carefully from both natural and supernatural forces.

PREGNANCY AND BIRTH

The seventh month of a pregnancy is celebrated on most islands with a ritual bath for the mother-to-be. On Java there is a ceremony where the pregnant woman prepares a special spicy fruit salad and "sells" it to guests who pay for it with roof tiles. It is believed the sale teaches frugality to the child and the taste of the salad indicates the baby's sex— sour for a boy and sweet for a girl.

Throughout her pregnancy the mother is given specially prepared food and not allowed to touch sharp objects, such as knives and scissors, which might "harm" the child. No gifts are given for an unborn child as overzealous actions and words are considered to invite evil.

Once the child is born it is guarded through its first five years. Every ethnic group has a different welcoming ceremony for the baby. In Java the destiny of the child is predicted by placing various objects like a book, pen and some gold in front of the child to see which object attracts its attention first. Special threads with amulets around the child's arms or neck protect it against evil and daily smears of special infant *jamu* (see page 119) keep the child safe.

THE GROWING-UP YEARS

Children are particularly treasured in Indonesia, not least because the country has one of the highest infant mortality rates in the world.

Babies are always kept slung comfortably and securely at the mother's hip in a long, narrow piece of *batik*, the *selandang*. A child can demand to be carried this way for several years, or at least until the arrival of the next child. In this *selandang* the child is fed according to its pangs of hunger rather than the clock.

Everyone in Indonesia has a certain status and knows his proper place. There is security in this knowledge and nobody wants to disturb the peace by upsetting this system. Children soon learn that, within the family, status is arranged in a hierarchical order according to age rather than sex, with the father being right at the top. He is always a somewhat distant figure to be honored rather than made a friend.

A child being carried in a *selandang*.

Years later this carries over to the "whatever pleases the boss" philosophy of most Indonesians. *Bapak* is the word for father and is also used for anyone senior in age or status. No effort is spared to please anyone occupying the father-figure position. The boss is only told what he wants to hear, true feelings and facts are covered up, and to argue with superiors is considered rude. Direct eye-contact may be misinterpreted as a challenge, so the Javanese speak to superiors with downcast eyes in as humble a stance as possible.

CIRCUMCISION

When Moslem boys reach the age of 11, they undergo circumcision to mark their passage into manhood. In the past, they would anesthetize themselves with icy cold water before the event. Today there are mass circumcisions using modern medical equipment in most villages. Sometimes the boys are dressed up as princes and paraded through town on ponies or decorated *becak* (three-wheeled pedicabs). A *selamatan* (see page 56) will usually follow.

A mass circumcision ceremony.

The child's attachment to an older relative—grandfather, cousin, aunt or uncle—grows stronger than the bond with his parents. Often the grandparents take full responsibility, financial and otherwise, for one grandchild. Children in turn help out with household chores, though a grandson is pampered more than a granddaughter and is only expected to run the occasional errand.

Children are only considered grown-up once they get married. Until then they live with their parents, help out financially with the household expenses and fulfill the social obligations expected of them. Once they get married, the bride either stays at her husband's home, or the couple gets a place of their own. It is only in the Minangkabau matrilineal system in West Sumatra that the reverse occurs.

The annual family reunion takes place at Lebaran when, just like at Christmas, everyone comes together from all parts of the archipelago to celebrate and exchange news.

MARRIAGE

In Indonesia everyone is expected to marry. In the rural areas the average age a person marries at is much lower than in the cities, and by the time a girl reaches the age of 19 she would be not only married but also a mother. The eternal Indonesian optimism shines through when even a 60-year-old bachelor replies to the question, "Are you married?" with a standard "*Belum*" meaning "Not yet." Moslem law permits a man to have up to four wives although this is not encouraged by the government.

There is no event as extravagant as a wedding, though occasionally funeral ceremonies surpass this (see page 62). The most elaborate ethnic costumes are worn and lavish gifts, including gold, money, fruit and flowers, are exchanged. The bride and groom sit in regal style on ornate thrones upon a raised platform and never mix with guests except to mumble a thank you when the guests file past to congratulate them. These wedding feasts, where the guests number anything from a few hundred to several thousand, often leave a family in debt.

The bride feeding the groom—a ritual during a Javanese wedding.

DEATH AND FUNERALS

A Moslem is buried within 24 hours of death and bus loads of colleagues, friends and relatives arrive within hours to pay respect to the deceased, regardless of how close they were. There is an air of self-control as weeping is not considered therapeutic but an indication of a weak soul and an invitation to spirits.

It is believed that when a person dies his spirit must be properly "managed" or it will cause havoc in the world of the living. To prevent the soul from returning to earth, some rites are designed to confuse it. In Sumatra the body is sent out of the house through a small gap in the floor which is then sealed. In Bali and Sulawesi the hearse is jolted and jarred to prevent the spirit from finding its way back. For the soul to successfully make it to the land of the ancestors—usually in the form of a bird or insect—proper funeral rites are essential. Although these vary by region and ethnic group, they are almost always colorful and extravagant spectacles.

If a family cannot afford this expense at the time of death, the body is either kept wrapped in shrouds in the house or temporarily buried till enough money is saved for the rites. In the recent death of a Toradjan royal person, the widow kept the embalmed body of her husband in the house for two years before having one of the most spectacular funerals ever. In Bali the bereaved wait for enough deaths to pool together resources for a joint cremation. The bones are then exhumed, cleaned and given a proper send off.

A Balinese royal cremation. Funerals are very often expensive affairs, especially in Bali where the dead are cremated in elaborate ceremonies.

Toradjanese houses, a replica of which is seen near the effigies of their dead, are shaped like canoes and all face north. Their ancestors are believed to have come from that direction in similar vessels which they later pulled ashore and used as roofs.

The dead are never forgotten in Indonesia: among the Toradjanese, eerie effigies of the dead line the cliff faces, their final burial place; the Irian Jayans preserve the skull and bones of the deceased; and, all over Indonesia, graves or symbolic statues are carefully tended, as they contain the benevolent spirits of ancestors.

RELIGION

AS FOUR OF THE FIVE GREAT "World Religions"—Hinduism, Buddhism, Islam and Christianity (the fifth being Judaism)—came across the seas they were absorbed into Indonesia. Yet none quite managed to erase the original animistic beliefs and traditional customs (*adat*) which had "come down from the mountains" and existed for centuries.

Religion has been laid down like a multi-layered cake in Indonesia, each layer interacting with but never quite replacing the one before it. The earliest inhabitants were animists, believing in spirit and ancestor worship and in the hidden powers of natural objects such as the mountains, trees, rice, rain and the sun. When Hinduism/Buddhism came to Indonesia, it intermingled with this animism. Then when Islam and Christianity arrived centuries later, these too were modified and adapted to fit in with the existing mixture of *adat*, animism and Hindu-Buddhist beliefs. It is said that in Indonesia it is easier to know when a religion started than when it ended.

Opposite: **Worshipers in prayer on the Hindu island of Bali.**

"Religion comes in from the sea, but customs come down from the mountains."

—*Indonesian proverb*

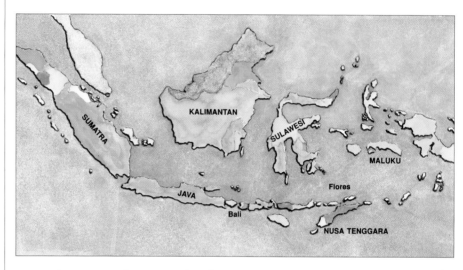

Map of Indonesia show-
ing the different religions
of its peoples.

In the spirit of *Pancasila*, there is complete freedom of worship, although everyone is expected to believe in the existence of a God. Religion is taken seriously and is an academic subject in school up to the second year of university.

Indonesia is the world's largest Islamic nation with 88% of its 178 million people registered as Moslems. Hinduism is confined mainly to the islands of Bali and Lombok, while Christianity is found in pockets throughout the archipelago.

ISLAM

When Arab traders brought Islam to Indonesia, it was quickly accepted and swept more or less peacefully through the islands, first along the trade routes and later inland.

Islam preached the equality and brotherhood of man, an idea which appealed to the common people who were tired of being at the bottom of the rigid, hierarchical Hindu caste system. The few communities which resisted conversion, like the Badui and the Toradjanese, fled to the interior as Islam encroached.

Islam is a way of life, a practical rather than merely theoretical religion. Today it pervades every aspect of Indonesian life: loudspeakered mosques call the faithful to prayer five times a day; Friday, the Islamic holy day, is a half-day; pigs are not very often found as they are seen as unclean; most public places have a little room set aside for prayer; public toilets provide a place to wash the feet but no toilet paper as water is considered cleaner and more hygienic; men are allowed to take more than one wife; and, many Indonesians save money to make the *haj* or holy journey to Mecca.

The national mosque of Indonesia is the Istiqlal Mosque in Jakarta.

Friday prayers at a mosque. Prayer is a very important part of a Moslem's life: he has to pray five times a day and on Friday, all men must go to the mosque for special prayers at mid-day.

The Islam practiced by individual communities ranges from the ultra-orthodox Acehnese to nominal Moslems like the Central Javanese whose practices are mingled with animism and Hindu-Javanese mysticism. For instance, when a person is ill, the *dukun* or folk doctor writes Islamic prayers on pieces of paper and dunks them in a glass of water for the patient to drink. Once drunk, the prayers supposedly fight the demon that is causing the illness.

Rarely does one see extreme conservatism in Indonesia. Women, for instance, are much freer than their sisters in other Islamic countries. Here they do not wear facial veils but a very flattering low-cut blouse with a colorful, figure-hugging *sarung* skirt instead. A husband has to get permission from his first wife before taking a second wife, and women are allowed to initiate divorce. In societies like the Minangkabau of Sumatra the matriarchal system exists in harmony with Islam's male-supremacy. In the big cities many women run successful businesses and are active in government.

THE CALL TO PRAYER

Moslems traditionally pray five times a day: at sunset, night, dawn, noon and afternoon. The prayer times are published in the papers, broadcast over radio and television and sounded in mosques all over the country.

There is a strict ritual before each prayer:

If it is Friday, you roll your prayer rug and take it to the nearest mosque. On other days only the men go to the mosque, the women pray at home.

You purify your body:

Wash the hands from the wrist down, gargle and spit to cleanse the mouth, wash the face and the lower arms up to the elbows, moisten part of the head, comb the hair with water, and finally wash both feet up to the ankles. All this is repeated three times in strict order and always starting with the right side. Menstruating women may not enter the mosque.

You purify your mind:

If a man touches a dog or a woman, goes to the bathroom or "passes wind" he must repeat the ritual cleansing. Women shroud themselves in a white gown from head to toe while the men wrap a *sarung* around their waist.

You remove your shoes outside the mosque. Inside you must be careful not to touch any person or object, especially not the Holy Koran.

You greet fellow worshipers with the words *As salaam 'alaikum* ("Peace be with you") and respond *Alaikum salaam* ("And upon you, peace").

The prayer begins.

HINDUISM

Hinduism is the oldest religion on earth, dating back to before 1000 B.C. When it arrived in Java, the religion made such an impact that its influence lingers today. The palaces of Solo and Yogyakarta are still hard-core cultural enclaves of this long gone period; the characters and stories of Javanese classical dance and puppetry are based on the ancient Hindu epics, the *Mahabharata* and *Ramayana*; numerous Hindu ruins and ancient monuments, like Prambanan, are scattered all over the island; the Garuda, the mount of Lord Vishnu the Preserver, is the national emblem; and Sanskrit, the language of Hinduism, abounds in Javanese and Indonesian words, place names and even the state motto, *Pancasila.*

However, Hinduism's greatest influence remains in Bali. It came here when the Majapahits fled from their homeland in Java to escape Moslem invaders. The rich Hindu-Javanese culture, religion and philosophy they brought with them were superimposed on existing Balinese animism, giving rise to today's unique Balinese Hinduism (see box).

BALI'S HINDUISM

Balinese Hinduism consists of deeply-rooted animism overlaid with a veneer of Hindu practices brought to Bali when the Majapahits fled Java. Traces of Hinduism can be seen in the Balinese belief in the Trinity of Gods—Brahma the Creator, Vishnu the Preserver and Shiva the Destroyer—and the all-important cremation of the dead to release the spirit, enabling it to participate in the cycle of reincarnation. Balinese names are a reflection of an earlier caste system and their knowledge of the Hindu epics forms the basis of their dance and other art forms.

Yet the Balinese practice ancestor worship, blood sacrifices and mysticism. They often go into trances and are possessed by the gods and demons surrounding them in nature. They have numerous rites and sacrifices—hardly a day goes by without a ceremony aimed at keeping peace with the forces of nature. In fact, these endless colorful and elaborate temple ceremonies have become a major tourist attraction.

A Balinese temple courtyard.

Devotees praying at the ancient monument of Borobudur.

BUDDHISM

Hinduism and Buddhism have coexisted on Java for over one thousand years. This coexistence has resulted in so much borrowing and adapting that it is sometimes difficult to distinguish between the two. Today, most Buddhists, such as the Chinese and Tenggerese, live in Java and congregate for their annual Waisak celebrations at Borobudur, the largest Buddhist monument in the world.

Left: A Catholic church in East Timor.

Below: The interior of an Indonesian church with its *batik*-inspired altar.

CHRISTIANITY

Despite being under colonial rule for decades, only 9% of Indonesia is Christian. The Christianity practiced by most ethnic groups, whether Protestant or Catholic, has been completely intermingled with local beliefs, producing some interesting customs like the barefoot Easter procession in the dead of night in Flores, *gamelan*-led masses in Yogyakarta, and bull-sacrifices among the Toradjanese Christians.

ANIMISM

For want of a better word, those without "religions" such as the Dayaks are called animists. Many hill folks and isolated communities continue to follow traditional ways of venerating ancestors and placating the spirits of nature although they are coming under increasing pressure to convert.

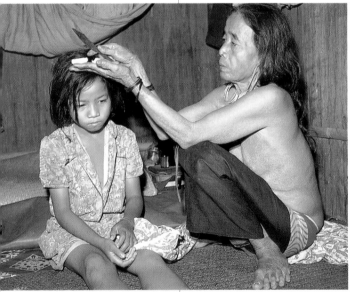

A lady shaman or witch doctor in Kalimantan curing a sick girl with an egg. It is believed the egg will "absorb" the "bad" spirits causing the illness within the girl.

GHOSTS AND GENIES In Java when children do not sleep, they are told of the dreadful *way-way*, the "frightener" of small children. In Sulawesi, it is the *pok-pok*, the flying head, while in Bali, they fear the *leyak*s who kidnap troublesome children.

Although these are only stories, Indonesians do believe in spirits and mysticism. Even the country's leaders seek that divine spirit called the *wahyu*, which enters a person to provide guidance, for major decisions.

Stories of ghosts, goddesses, demons, spirits and genies abound everywhere. Buffalo heads are placed in the foundations of all new buildings to appease the spirits, with priests often flying sacrificial heads by helicopter to offshore oil rigs for the same purpose. Witch doctors exorcise evil from temples, swimming pools, cars and hotels. And any transition in life—birth, circumcision, marriage, death—is accompanied by dramatic rituals and elaborate meals in the traditional *selamatan* (see page 56) ceremony.

A spirit figure. Many Indonesians often own talismans and spirit figures to protect them from "evil."

Trees, flowers, hair, fingernails, blood and secret weapons like the *keris* (dagger) all possess a "life force." These must be handled and disposed of with caution. Some communities worship stones, others sacrifice animals to volcanoes or perform trance dances. The island of Bali is so full of wandering supernatural beings that its nickname "The Enchanted Isle" takes on a new meaning!

And every Indonesian fears the Queen of the South Seas, the spiritual wife of the Sultan of Yogyakarta, who seizes anyone wearing a green swimsuit to become a soldier in her army. Most hotels along the south coast of Java keep one room locked and specially reserved for whenever she should visit.

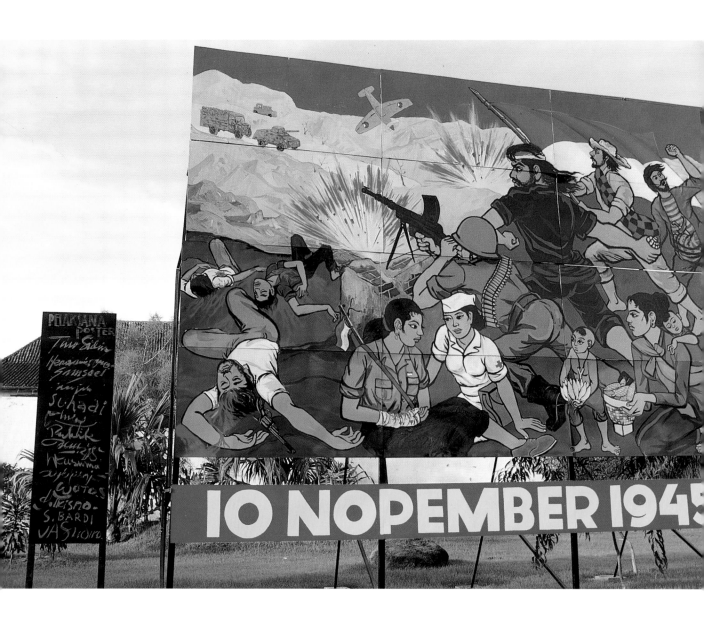

LANGUAGE

"ONE PEOPLE, ONE LANGUAGE, ONE NATION"

IN A LAND OF great ethnic diversity, it is not surprising that there are at least 300 languages in Indonesia. And that's not counting the numerous dialects within each language. For instance, Sulawesi alone has 62 documented languages and countless more dialects.

With such linguistic variety it is easy to see why the Indonesian motto, *Bhinneka Tunggal Ika* (Unity in Diversity) is most relevant in the world of language. Bahasa Indonesia was the language carefully chosen in 1928 to bridge the linguistic gap between the scattered islands. Today it is the cultural element which unifies them.

The second most widely spoken language is Javanese. Dutch is used by those over 40, but today English is the first foreign language taught in schools. Very few people speak English, however, as there is little opportunity to use the language and the few stilted phrases learned are soon forgotten.

Opposite: **Many foreign words have been adopted into Bahasa Indonesia. For example, the month of November is** *Nopember.*

BAHASA INDONESIA For centuries Malay had been the language of trade throughout the archipelago. Yet when nationalist leaders talked about freedom in the early 20th century, it was in Dutch, the language of the oppressors. This embarrassing irony made them realize that a common language was an essential vehicle of national unity. In the famous "Youth Pledge" of 1928 three ideals were adopted: One Fatherland, Indonesia; One Nation, Indonesia; and, One Language, Bahasa Indonesia, the language of unity.

When the Japanese arrived in the 1940's, they also actively encouraged Bahasa Indonesia, using it to spread Japanese propaganda throughout the archipelago. Their efforts were very successful. Bahasa Indonesia became so widespread that after independence there was no question of changing the national language.

Bahasa Indonesia (literally, "the language of Indonesia") is rated as one of the simplest languages in the world. It has no tenses, grammatical gender, tones or articles, and its few plurals are made by simply repeating the word. It is easy to learn the language for simple communication, although the refined variety with its complex affix structure and strict grammatical rules is less accessible. It is a democratic language, without the status markers present in Javanese, Sundanese and Balinese (see box). And most importantly, it is a neutral language as it does not belong to any particular ethnic group. Choosing Javanese, for instance, would have discriminated against those in the outer islands.

A welcome sign in an airport. The column on the left is in Bahasa Indonesia while the message is translated in English on the right.

The long history of contact between Indonesia and the rest of the world is reflected in the large number of loan words in Bahasa Indonesia. There are over 7,000 Dutch words (for example *meubel* for furniture); Portuguese words (the island of Flores is Portuguese for flowers); English words (*doktor* and *opisboi* for doctor and office boy); and numerous Sanskrit, Arabic, Polynesian, Tagalog, Chinese, French, Javanese and Spanish words as well.

THE LANGUAGE OF HIERARCHY

Imagine a language so complex that to say the words "to say," one has five choices: *kandha, sanjang, criyos, matur* or *ngendika*. The word used depends on the "level" of speech chosen. And the level depends on who is speaking to whom, their relative ages and status, the situation, the sex, generation and race of the speaker and so on.

The three levels of speech are *Ngoko, Madya* and *Krama,* and each has different words for everyday things. *Ngoko* is the first language a child learns. It is simple, unrefined, familiar and used between close friends. The highest level is *Krama*, an elegant and polite speech used in formal situations. In between the familiar and the formal is *Madya* speech, used when people of low status talk or when two close friends speak respectfully. In addition there is low *Krama* and high *Krama* to indicate the status of the speakers, and other levels of speech used only for royalty and ritual feasts.

This complex, hierarchical language has been heavily influenced by the Indian caste system, where everyone has and must be addressed according to a certain rank. To use the wrong word would be insulting and to operate on the wrong level disastrous—no wonder the Javanese find it easier to speak in Bahasa Indonesia!

BODY LANGUAGE

In general Indonesians tend to be much more reserved in their body movements and gestures than westerners. Unnecessarily flinging the arms, jerking the head and talking loudly (even in anger) is considered *kasar* or "unrefined." The nuances caught in facial expressions, gestures and other body signals often say as much, if not more, than the message in the words alone.

Here is a short list of body language peculiar to Indonesians:

THE HEAD AND THE FEET The head and the feet are, by virtue of their position, the most and least esteemed parts of the body respectively. The head contains the "life force" and is thus considered sacred. In the past, head-hunters (like the Dayaks of Kalimantan and Toradjanese of Sulawesi) would bring back enemy heads for good luck. Today, children are never patted on the head. Respect is also shown by keeping the head lower than the person being honored.

One has to be just as careful with one's feet: pointing them at someone is disrespectful, and propping them up on a table is absolutely taboo.

GREETING In greetings there is no effusive hugging and kissing, just a respectful Islamic "handshake" where you hold both the hands of the other person, let go, and then bring your hands to your chest. In social circles, however, the ladies kiss each other on both cheeks Dutch-style.

The Islamic "handshake."

80

STANDING In most situations Indonesians tend to stand in what is considered the most humble and respectful stance: the hands lightly overlapped in front of the body, the head slightly bowed and if talking to someone of higher status, the eyes lowered. Standing with the hands on the hips is aggressive and when held behind the back, considered too superior.

WALKING When in a restricted space one asks permission before walking in front of someone. This is done by bending low, extending the right arm forward, mumbling a *permisi* ("please give me permission," that is, excuse me) and quickly walking across.

POINTING Indonesians only point with their thumb. Using any other finger is considered rude. The gesture is like a gentler version of that used in America for hitching a ride, but with a more open palm. This gesture is also used like a "go ahead" signal when asking someone to proceed. For instance one would use it to invite someone to start on a meal by pointing at the food.

Pointing the Indonesian way to invite a guest to have a cup of coffee.

GESTURES Rude or obscene signs are seldom seen. One different gesture is the one indicating madness. Instead of circling the index finger at the forehead, the hand is used to "saw" the forehead in two: "you half-brain!"

SMILING The smile is ever-present in Indonesia, but it does not always indicate happiness. The Javanese are known to giggle when they are sad, smile when they have to give bad news, and laugh when nervous or confused. Some of these differences are related to their belief that life should remain as calm and unruffled as possible.

ARTS

THE ROYAL TRADITION

INDONESIA has a great variety of both folk and classical arts. Most of these have three things in common: they are an integral part of traditional life; they have been heavily influenced by ancient Chinese and Hindu civilizations; and, lastly, many were limited to the Javanese courts.

The secrets of *gamelan* music, *wayang* drama and age-old *batik*-making used to be strictly royal traditions. Until recently, these arts were either pursued by ladies of the nobility or by specially commissioned artists only. The royal monopoly on classical dance, for instance, was not broken till 1918 when the first school was set up outside the palace walls.

Left: **A Balinese dancer in full concentration.**

Opposite: **The colorful wooden puppets used in *wayang golek*.**

A *gamelan* orchestra—the music of art, religion and government in Indonesia. Since its introduction to the west in the 19th century, it has been recognized as one of the world's most sophisticated musical arts.

MUSIC

Gamelan has been described as "the sound of moonlight." It sounds marvelously fluid, something between jazz and the gentle rippling of water. It has no written score and is taught informally from generation to generation. It dates back to at least the 10th century A.D., when it was depicted on Borobudur reliefs.

Today, *gamelan* accompanies dance, theater and royal and religious festivities. It even appears in mosques in clear violation of Islamic law but in keeping with Javanese *adat*. There are two distinct versions: the slow, stately, measured Javanese *gamelan* and the Balinese version which explodes with energy and vibrancy.

This percussion ensemble can have anything between five and forty instruments. It is arranged like a tree with the "roots" (bronze gongs providing the low, sturdy support), the "trunk" (metalophones—bronze, brass or iron percussion instruments—of various sizes providing the basic melody) and the "leaves" and "branches" which are the *gamelan*'s complex ornamentation. This is all controlled by the "conductors," wooden drums which provide the cues.

An *angklung* orchestra.

Unlike most western instruments, *gamelan* has a unique two-scale tuning method. This means every set has a distinctive sound based on the preference of the maker. Unfortunately, the tremendous transport costs mean *gamelan* music is seldom heard outside Indonesia. Nevertheless, its recurrent rhythmic melody has inspired the avant-garde western "minimalistic" music movement associated with composers such as Claude Debussy and Philip Glass.

THE *ANGKLUNG*

The *angklung* is a simple portable instrument made of two rows of hollow bamboo tubes of various lengths suspended in a frame. This frame is shaken to produce a strange xylophonic sound. In the old days it was used to march into battle. Today it is a must in all school ensembles.

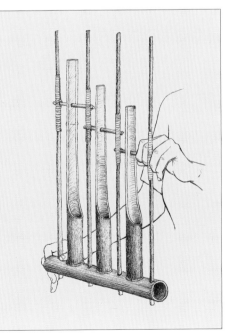

"There is something so extremely simple, and at the same time gay, in the sound produced by the rattling of these bamboo tubes, that I confess I have never heard the angklung without pleasure."

—*Sir Stamford Raffles, in A History of Java*

DANCE

The *kuda kepang* or hobby-horse trance dance. The spirit of the horses enters the dancers to give them extraordinary powers.

Opposite top: **Balinese temple dancers.**

Opposite bottom: **Young women being trained in classical Javanese dance.**

In Indonesia, dance is closely associated with rituals like exorcising of spirits, performing rites of passage ceremonies such as birth, circumcision and death, and celebrating various agricultural events.

Traditional dance is riddled with ritual, storytelling and trance. Bali's trance dances are famous and, in Java, there is a hobby-horse dance where the dancers absorb the spirit and mannerisms of the horses they ride. They then perform unusual feats including eating light bulbs.

Traditional and folk dances are vibrant, energetic and require little formal training, but the famous classical dances of Java and Bali are quite the opposite. This dance tradition still retains some of its Indian origins: bent knees, turned-out legs, straight body with head tilted to one side

and the use of hand gestures. Training starts when the child is six years old. It often takes years to achieve just one gesture such as the arching of the fingers backward to touch the forearm.

Javanese classical dance is serene, controlled and subtle. This reflects a true courtly style. The dancer's eyes are always downcast, the limbs kept close to the body and there are long silent hypnotizing pauses. However, Balinese dance, like everything else in Bali, explodes with energy. The dancers burst onto the stage, often to the sound of gongs and cymbals, with eyes agape, arms held high and often darting around in a manner that totally startles the subdued Javanese.

DRAMA AND PUPPETRY

Drama in Indonesia is usually in the form of puppetry. *Wayang*, as it is called, is more than a mere spectacle on stage and is probably the most powerful cultural force in the country. It indirectly teaches about life and all its contradictions, imparts moral values and even provides heroic role-models for the young. Its characters are often used to describe personalities: an Ardjuna is a good-looking, confident and loyal person; Rahwana implies deception, evil and greed; and Semar, one of the oldest and most respected characters, is a truly honorable name to give someone.

Wayang has such an impact that it is also used for spreading government-sponsored statements to the villages. Its performances are exciting, all-night affairs. When a traveling troupe arrives in a village, the entire community gathers to watch.

The rules of this theater are very different from western theater. The atmosphere is noisy and informal where entire families—from grand-mothers to babes-in-arms—relax on mats on the floor and only half-watch the show; everyone is familiar with the ancient stories. Instead they socialize, catch up on gossip, disappear to have something to eat and doze off when tired only to be awakened by the gongs heralding the exciting battle scenes. All this continues into the early hours of the morning when everyone returns home tired but happy, full of the wonderful stories of "brave heroes and great kingdoms."

A *wayang kulit* or shadow puppet.

The most popular types of drama are *wayang topek* (masked drama), *wayang kulit* (shadow puppetry), *wayang golek* (wooden puppetry) and *wayang orang* (dance drama). Each of these is a regional specialty and depicts different stories and legends.

"There are those who watch the shadow play, weeping and sad in their foolish understanding, knowing full well that it is really only carved leather which moves and speaks."

—11th century Javanese poem

A performance of *wayang kulit* (shadow puppetry). The puppeteers sit behind the screen to "tell" their stories.

ART AND CRAFT

TEXTILES Traditional Indonesian textiles—primitive bark cloth, woven *ikat*, silk *songket* and sophisticated *batik*—are often treated as highly sacred ritualistic or religious objects. Painstakingly woven *ikat* are used to swaddle the dead, intricately dyed *batik* is wrapped around a bridal couple to symbolize unity, and the sacred *maa* cloth of the Toradjanese is used only for rituals.

The most famous are the Sumatran "ship cloths," which depict a scene reminiscent of Noah's Ark with angular-armed people, plants and animals. These are used to wrap a newborn child, and then for every successive significant event in that child's life, until finally he is buried in it.

To produce one labor-intensive woven *ikat*—from the auspicious day the thread is ritualistically mounted onto the loom till the day the textile is completed—can take up to ten years. *Ikat* is the fabric produced by a traditional method of weaving with areas of threads tied off to create a

Above: The *canting* is a small bamboo scoop used to draw designs for *batik*.

Left: The manufacture of *batik* involves the drawing of a design in melted wax with a *canting*.

Below: Silver and gold threads are used in the weaving of elaborate silken *songket*.

design. Today these much sought-after textiles command a high price.

Another type of textile production which requires extraordinary patience is *batik*. This age-old art has been perfected by the Javanese, who produce the finest *batik* in the world. The intricacy of this art is achieved with the hand-held *canting*, which is used to draw fine wax patterns such as stylized human and animal figures on fabric. The cloth is then dyed to color the non-waxed areas and the process is repeated until the brilliant detail typical of *batik* is obtained. However, a cheaper and faster printing-block method is becoming more popular today.

Batik designs used to be deeply symbolic with some being reserved only for royal use. Today, there are over a thousand designs with twenty regional styles and countless color combinations.

Above: **An example of perishable Balinese art—intricate palm leaf weavings used for temple festivals.**

Right: **A Balinese artist hard at work in one of the many studios found on the island.**

BALI'S ART When they say, "Everyone in Bali is an artist," they are not exaggerating. For its size, Bali produces an awe-inspiring output of quality art. The island's sculptors produce everything from slim, elegant ebony rice-goddesses to fierce, bulging stone demons which guard all of Bali's crossroads and bridges.

The Balinese have been avid painters for the last 400 years. Their original two-dimensional paintings have now moved into three dimensions, often with a blaze of colors and dozens of myths and stories happening simultaneously on the canvas.

Most of Bali's art is perishable, however—intricate palm-leaf offerings which wither by day's end or artfully layered cones of food balanced precariously on women's heads to and from the temples.

THE MAGIC *KERIS*

The traditional handcrafted wavy-bladed dagger is believed to possess a spirit imbibed by its maker. These magical daggers—over 40 varieties exist—are shrouded in mystery and secret powers. It is believed they can talk, walk, fly and even kill a person by simply piercing his footprint. They can warn of danger by rattling in their sheaths, relieve a woman's labor pains and even avert floods. And if a groom is unable to be present at his marriage, he is represented by his *keris*. They can bring both good and bad luck; so they are ceremoniously cleaned and wrapped in precious silks and generally taken very good care of by their owners.

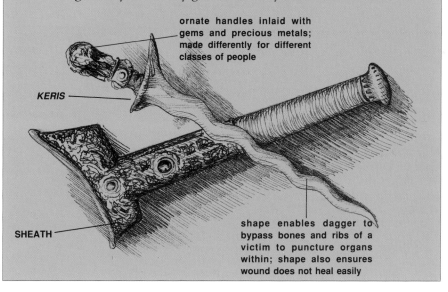

ornate handles inlaid with gems and precious metals; made differently for different classes of people

KERIS

SHEATH

shape enables dagger to bypass bones and ribs of a victim to puncture organs within; shape also ensures wound does not heal easily

LEISURE

SUNDAYS ARE FUNDAYS

IN INDONESIA, Sundays are strictly for leisure. Nowhere is this more obvious than in Jakarta, where traffic is diverted from the main roads to make way for the hoards of residents who stream onto the empty streets for recreation. From the first break of daylight, the streets are filled with children and teenagers playing, dancing or listening to music, skaters and cyclists, marchers preparing for a parade, vendors, babes-in-arms—just about everyone joins in and enjoys this weekly fiesta.

Opposite: **A grease pole competition, a traditional game still enjoyed in Kalimantan.**

Below: **One of the main streets in Jakarta closed for a parade.**

95

TRADITIONAL GAMES AND SPORTS

There are numerous traditional games associated with the different islands of Indonesia.

In Nias, young men enjoy the frightening sport of stone-jumping. The aim is to clear a thick stone wall about five feet high and one-and-a-half feet wide, sometimes with a sword in hand. After running about 22 yards up to the wall, the men jump high into the air, always landing feet first on the other side. These walls, once covered with sharp spikes, were used to train warriors to jump enemy walls with a torch in one hand and a sword in the other.

Indonesia is also a nation of sea-farers and proud boat-makers: today, boat racing is a colorful tradition on several islands. Balinese men enjoy the sport of cock fighting, while the Madurese spend long hours preparing their sleek bulls for their annual bull races (see page 108).

A demonstration of *pencak silat,* a form of martial arts.

Some sports span the islands. *Sepak tekrau,* which resembles volleyball, is an energetic game where two teams try to keep a rattan ball in the air with their feet. Another sport, *pencak silat,* is actually a martial art which originated in Sumatra where priests observed and copied the graceful yet lethal movements of animals. When it spread to the royal houses of Java, its deft movements were refined and perfected. Today youth of both sexes train themselves in this art.

Almost every Indonesian has spent many wonderful hours playing the leisurely game of *congkak,* where shells or pebbles are placed in a certain order into depressions on a wooden board. This game is considered a must at all family gatherings.

MODERN GAMES AND SPORTS

The government's motto "Sport for All" aims to achieve a nation of sports-minded people. Every year a National Sports Day is held on September 9 and participants from around the archipelago gather for a week of friendly competition. In the early days of the event, before Indonesia had gained international recognition as an independent nation, these games stood as a symbol of Indonesia's internal unity to the outside world.

The most popular sports are badminton and soccer. Indonesians have held the coveted Thomas Cup for badminton since 1958, except for three years when China captured the trophy. And Rudy Hartono has become something of a living legend for winning the "All-England" badminton championship eight times.

Boxing and tennis are also extremely popular, though the expenses involved in the latter put it out of the reach of many. Indonesia's prized boxer, Ellyas Pical, has won international acclaim, while the nation's tennis team has brought home many of the regional trophies. During the 1988 Olympic Games in Seoul, the women's archery team did Indonesia proud by winning its first Olympic medal since the country joined the Games in 1952.

Rudy Hartono during an All-England badminton final. He is the undisputed king of the game, having won the championship eight times.

FESTIVALS

LAND OF ALL YEAR-AROUND FESTIVITIES

IN BALI, there are endless colorful temple anniversaries or *odalan*, religious holidays and passage of life ceremonies which involve the whole community. On the island of Java, great traditional festivals are held by the royal courts on Islamic holidays. In other parts of Indonesia, there are harvest and sea festivals which are a mixture of local traditions and religious beliefs. Cities and towns also celebrate their anniversaries with sports events, traditional art performances and, sometimes, processions.

The actual day of each festival is calculated according to local calendars. The European calendar is based on the solar year of 365 days, whereas the Moslems base theirs on the lunar year of 354 days. Thus their festivals "move back" by about 11 days every solar year. The Balinese and other ethnic groups calculate their calendars in other ways. Thus the dates of festivals cannot be forecast far in advance. This is also true for the 12 official holidays, which tend to be Java-oriented. As Indonesia is the world's largest Moslem nation, a large proportion of the official holidays are Islamic.

Opposite: **Balinese women entering a temple gateway, their heads laden with offerings for a temple anniversary.**

THE 12 OFFICIAL HOLIDAYS

Jan 1	New Year's Day
	Nyepi (Hindu New Year)
	Good Friday
	Isra Mi'raj Nabi Muhamad (Ascension of the Prophet Mohammed)
	The Ascension of Christ
	Waisak
	Lebaran
Aug 17	Independence Day
	Idul Adha (Day of Sacrifice)
	Hegira (Moslem New Year)
	Gareberg (Prophet Mohammed's Birthday)
Dec 25	Christmas

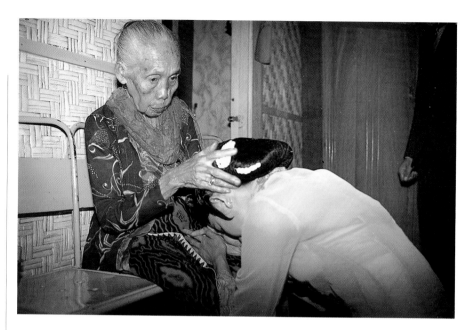

ISLAMIC FESTIVALS

Lebaran, or the Arabic Idul Fitri, is by far the most important festival in Indonesia, just as Christmas is for much of the western world.

For one month before Lebaran, Moslems fast from dawn until sunset. This is the month of *Ramadan* when children and adults alike do not eat or drink anything during the day as a test of their spiritual values and self-

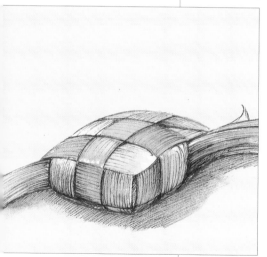

discipline. Lebaran marks the end of *Ramadan* and is celebrated by noisy festivity throughout the archipelago. People wear new clothes, light fire-crackers, prepare elaborate meals at home and visit friends and relatives bearing gifts of specially prepared cakes and cookies.

This is also the time for the young to ask forgiveness for any wrong-doings committed intentionally or unintentionally through the year. The greeting *Selamat Idul Fitri: Ma'afkan Lahir Batin* ("Happy Lebaran and May You Forgive All Our Wrongs and Unexpressed Hostile Sentiments") can be heard from every home.

Lebaran lasts a whole month. Streets are filled with people selling colorful cakes and the traditional *ketupat* (a small woven palm-leaf container in which steamed rice is prepared for serving to guests) for the initial two days.

Gareberg commemorates the birthday of the Prophet Mohammed and is marked by the biggest religious procession held in the Islamic center of Java. Two days before Gareberg, large ceremonial food mounds are painstakingly prepared at the royal palace during the Tumplak Wajik Festival. During Gareberg these mounds are taken in a procession to the main mosque of the city, where they are blessed and distributed to the waiting people. A piece of the *gunungan* or food mound is believed to ensure good fortune and eternal youth as well as guarantee good harvests.

Isra Mi'raj Nabi Muhamad, the "Ascension of the Prophet Mohammed," celebrates the night when the Archangel Gabriel took the Prophet to heaven to speak with God.

Idul Adha is the festival of sacrifice when cattle and goats are slaughtered to signify Abraham's sacrifice of his son Isaac. This is when the faithful take a pilgrimage around the *Kaabah* in Mecca. In Indonesia, the graves of ancestors are also visited and cleaned during Idul Adha.

Hegira, the Islamic New Year, celebrates the day in A.D. 622 when Mohammed moved from Mecca to start a new community in Medina. In the Moslem calendar this move is commemorated by the letter H appearing after the year, for example 1302H.

Above: **The Hindu festival of Nyepi is the biggest celebration on Bali.**

Opposite: **Offerings (top) and temple decorations (bottom) for the Balinese festival of Galungan.**

HINDU FESTIVALS

Nyepi, the Hindu New Year, or the Day of Complete Silence, is spent in prayer and meditation. No fires are lit, no work or travel done and no one leaves the home.

The eve of Nyepi, in contrast, is one of the noisiest days on the Hindu island of Bali. First, offerings of wine and meat are laid at every crossroad to appease the demons believed to reside there. Then, as darkness falls, everyone comes out onto the streets and uses loud gongs, cymbals and

flaming torches to chase away any remaining demons.

Having thus chased away the evil spirits, the next day is spent in total silence, *nyepi*, in the hope that any returning demons will be tricked into believing that Bali is deserted and will go away.

Galungan is another important festive period in Bali, although it is not one of the official Indonesian holidays. These are ten days when the gods and revered ancestors return to earth. The Balinese spend long hours making intricate decorations and place these at roadsides and entrances of temples and homes as offerings. In the temples, the most elaborate and exciting religious productions take place simultaneously throughout the island of Bali.

BUDDHIST FESTIVALS

Waisak, the most important festival for the Buddhists, celebrates the three most significant moments of the life of Buddha, founder of the religion—his birth, his moment of enlightenment and his death.

Thousands gather at the monumental 1,000-year-old Borobudur temple in Central Java for this annual celebration. Here, a solemn procession of monks carrying flowers and reciting prayers winds its way around the terraces up to the main stupa in what is called the "Noble Silence." Offerings of fresh fruit and flowers are laid out at an ornately decorated altar.

The event climaxes when the moon reaches its fullest. Thousands of devotees and monks will light candles, meditate, and then recite holy verses.

CHRISTIAN FESTIVALS

Christmas is celebrated in the traditional manner in Indonesia but Easter is celebrated in an unusual way on the island of Flores.

Wearing dark clothes, triangular white hoods and costumes reminiscent of 16th century Portugal, the Christians form a barefoot procession through the streets of Flores at midnight. They carry a statue of the Virgin Mary, which is said to have been washed ashore many years ago, and a symbolic black coffin of Jesus to the beat of muffled drums. With the fire-lit torches and candles and grass pom-poms waving in the air, the procession is an eerie, though exciting, one to watch.

The midnight Easter procession on the predominantly Christian island of Flores.

The annual Bull Races of Madura are held during the months of August or September. It all began when plow teams raced over the length of a rice field. Today's racing bulls are specially bred and represent a source of regional pride, and are never used for plowing.

NON-RELIGIOUS FESTIVALS

The Bull Races of Madura are colorful and exciting events which take place after the harvest season. The bulls raced are fed a diet of chilli peppers, honey, beer and raw eggs. On the day of the race, they are brilliantly dressed and paraded through town. Once they reach the stadium, they are raced at speeds of over 30 miles per hour down the 110-yard track with their jockeys perched behind on wooden sleds. Finally, the victorious bull is proudly trotted home to be used as a stud.

The Kesodo Festival is held at the Bromo volcano in East Java. Every year, thousands of mountain-dwelling Tenggerese people from the surrounding countryside make a 14-day pilgrimage to Bromo. On the day of Kesodo, they gather at midnight to sacrifice chickens, goats and other market produce into the gaping, rumbling molten vent in order to placate the God of Bromo.

Legend has it that the first ancestor of the Tenggerese sacrificed his 25th child to the volcano god in return for an abundance of both crops

and children. Today, those who make the pilgrimage to Bromo ask for both protection from eruptions and good harvests for the coming year.

Kartini Day is a day set aside to honor Raden Ajeng Kartini (1879-1904), Indonesia's first woman liberator and one of the country's most-honored national heroes. Kartini fought against not only the restrictive Javanese *adat* (customs) system, but also for the right of women to be educated.

Today, parades, lectures and various school activities are held in her honor. They are attended by women throughout Indonesia, who wear their different regional dresses to symbolize the unity of the nation's women. Also, as on Mother's Day in the west, women are not allowed to work at home, as children and fathers take over household chores.

Every August 17 the people of Indonesia celebrate their Independence Day. Twenty-seven boys and girls, representing the different provinces, receive from the President a replica of the flag that was hoisted that same day in 1945 on the front steps of the Freedom Palace.

109

FOOD

CROSSROADS CUISINE

BEING AT THE CROSSROADS of the ancient trade routes, Indonesia has had an incredible mixture of foreign influences, especially in its cuisine. Numerous other cultures have borrowed and lent so much to the food that today there is no such thing as a "typical" Indonesian taste or flavor. From India came curries and turmeric, from the Chinese stir-frying and the indispensable *wok*, from the Arabs it was *kebab* and other mutton dishes, and the Europeans introduced carrots, tomatoes, pineapple and cauliflower, still referred to by their Dutch names.

Opposite: **Chillies or red peppers are an essential ingredient in Indonesian cooking.**

Below: **A dry-goods vendor displaying his wares of crackers and chips.**

Sate, skewered strips of marinated meat grilled over an open charcoal fire, is served with a peanut sauce and cut cucumbers and onions.

FAVORITE FOOD

Rice predominates in Indonesian cuisine. It is eaten three times a day, for breakfast, lunch and dinner. It is also turned into a colorful variety of snacks and sweets, eaten as the ever-popular *nasi goreng* or "fried rice" and even served in American-style fast-food restaurants.

Other favorites are soybean cake (*tahu*) and fermented soy beans wrapped in banana leaf (*tempe*). These are cheap and so rich in protein that they are called the "vegetarian meat" of the poor. Fish, poultry and eggs are preferred over red meats.

Indonesians have also perfected dishes from parts of plants we could never imagine are edible: the leaves of the bamboo, mango, papaya, cassava, cashew nut, and even the hibiscus; the flower of the banana tree; and an incredible variety of nuts and seeds.

Coconut is an ingredient typical of most Indonesian dishes. Apart from adding richness to curries and sauces, there are also a countless number of preparations which may be made with this humble fruit. Another favorite is a spicy peanut sauce which is poured over salads and accompanies traditional *sate* (skewered strips of marinated meat grilled over charcoal).

Most Indonesian food is either notoriously hot or accompanied by a fiery red chilli paste called *sambal*. The preparation of this scorching sauce varies regionally and often forms the standard by which a young girl's culinary skills are judged.

It is ironic though that the traditional spices (nutmeg, pepper, mace and cloves), which gave this region the name "The Spice Islands" and in search of which Columbus discovered America, do not figure prominently in Indonesian cuisine. Instead the delicate flavor of fresh herbs such as lemon grass, candle nut and basil are more popular.

Intricate rice offerings may be considered works of art.

THE IMPORTANCE OF RICE

Rice is not just the staple food of Indonesia but is the very symbol of life. Images of the rice goddess, two triangles woven from palm leaves or shaped with colored rice dough, are seen everywhere.

From planting until harvest, the crop is nurtured as one would look after a little child. It is believed that any carelessness will startle and chase away its sacred soul, Dewi Sri, resulting in crop failure.

During harvesting there is a tradition of hiding the cutting blade in the hand and mumbling apologies to Dewi Sri so that she does not "see" she is being violated, and forgives you even if she does.

Most fertility rites involve rice, with inverted cones of colored rice being essential for any ceremony to be complete. During major religious festivals enormous decorated mountains of rice are distributed and either eaten or left in the fields to ensure a plentiful harvest.

And only in Indonesia does a university professor's salary include a 10-pound sack of rice.

DRINK

Indonesian beverages are as varied as they are colorful, and some are elaborate enough to pass as desserts. Favorites are creamy fresh avocado juice, clear sweet perfumed Java tea, thick black *kopi tubruk* (which literally means "collision coffee," aptly named since it is prepared by pouring boiling water onto ground coffee) and fresh young coconut with the top sliced off and a straw inserted to get at the refreshing water within. Alcohol is seldom taken, being forbidden to Moslems, although non-Moslem communities do have strong brews of their own. And perhaps the most interesting of all Indonesian drinks is *Es Teler* (see box).

ES TELER, THE KING OF DRINKS

Es Teler is made differently all over Indonesia but a typical glass will have some or all of the following ingredients:

water
condensed milk
syrup
pieces of avocado
coconut shavings
red tapioca bits (shaped like pomegranate seeds)
cubes of sweetbread
gelatine
sweet corn
boiled red beans
crushed iced watermelon juice
mango . . . and numerous other nameless coagulated
    brightly-colored pulpy substances.

FRUIT

There is an amazing array of tropical fruit in Indonesia. Here are some which you may never have seen, much less tasted.

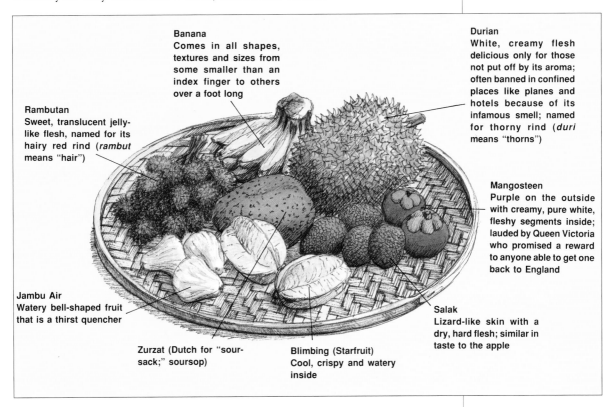

Banana
Comes in all shapes, textures and sizes from some smaller than an index finger to others over a foot long

Durian
White, creamy flesh delicious only for those not put off by its aroma; often banned in confined places like planes and hotels because of its infamous smell; named for thorny rind (*duri* means "thorns")

Rambutan
Sweet, translucent jelly-like flesh, named for its hairy red rind (*rambut* means "hair")

Mangosteen
Purple on the outside with creamy, pure white, fleshy segments inside; lauded by Queen Victoria who promised a reward to anyone able to get one back to England

Jambu Air
Watery bell-shaped fruit that is a thirst quencher

Salak
Lizard-like skin with a dry, hard flesh; similar in taste to the apple

Zurzat (Dutch for "sour-sack;" soursop)

Blimbing (Starfruit)
Cool, crispy and watery inside

Above: **A Bugis feast. The
food is placed in the
middle and the diner
helps himself to what he
feels like eating.**

TABLE MANNERS

Indonesians always invite others present to eat with them before starting
on a meal. To eat without giving a thought to others is considered most
uncivilized. Guests are always honored with special treatment. If they are
present, the table is laden with far more food than the guests can possibly
eat and that the host can realistically afford.

There are rules of etiquette for guests too. Foreign visitors quickly
learn "The Patience Game:" you should wait patiently until given the "go
ahead" by the host before eating or drinking anything. You also never
finish what is offered because, if you do, it means you are not satisfied
with what is offered and want more.

All the dishes are brought to the table together and everyone helps himself to a mound of rice and then samples one dish at a time. In rural areas, the food is placed on a large woven mat in the center of the kitchen with everyone sitting cross-legged around it.

Indonesians prefer eating with their fingers, believing the food is tastier than when using a fork and spoon. But they only use their right hand to eat as the left is considered unclean.

A host and guest eating with their fingers on the front porch of a house in Sumba.

117

Although Indonesia is a predominantly Moslem country, many of its people, who are not Moslems, eat pork.

FOOD BELIEFS AND TABOOS

The Moslem population does not eat pork as they consider the pig unclean. They also generally avoid alcohol. During the fasting month of *Ramadan* there is complete abstinence from both food and water from dawn to dusk, when prayers announce the break-of-fast.

Visitors, however, are often more surprised by what Indonesians *do* eat rather than what they do not. In some regions there is no taboo against eating dog meat, mice, eels and roasted lizards. In other regions they consume *tretis* (partially digested grass from the cow's stomach), dried pork and chicken blood, fried animal skins and intestines and curious looking offal. Many of these are regarded regional delicacies.

A *jamu* girl with her products walking along a Jakarta street. Interested buyers will stop her to buy whatever they need.

THE POWERS OF JAMU

Traditional herbal remedies, collectively called *jamu,* are very popular with Indonesians. These pastes, powders, creams and capsules are consumed daily and used to cure everything from headaches and fatigue to leprosy and flabby tummies.

This fascinating "nature cure" originated in the royal courts of Yogyakarta and Solo. Here, the ladies of the nobility spent their time discovering and perfecting the science of using roots, flowers, barks, nuts, herbs and spices to retain their beauty and vigor.

Today the ancient ancestral recipes are used to commercially manufacture an endless variety of *jamu* to sell to convinced customers.

EATING OUT

Indonesians often stop a *kaki lima* vendor to prepare a meal on the spot, visit a roadside *warung*, squat on mats on the pavement for traditional *gudeg*, or choose from a table laden with dishes in a Padang restaurant.

THE *KAKI LIMA* Pedestrian walks were officially built five feet wide, and today *kaki lima* (literally "five-foot way") refers to the hundreds of food vendors plying along them. These colorful vendors have become something of an institution, each with his or her characteristic cry or sound from a rattle of brass bells to the beating of a Chinese wooden block. The vendor summoned lowers his wares, carried on huge upward-curving bamboo yokes, squats in front of you, fans his charcoal brazier to a glow, and quickly cooks a dozen sticks of *sate* or a bowl of noodles.

MALIOBORO, THE LONGEST RESTAURANT IN THE WORLD

What is claimed to be the longest restaurant in the world can be found in Yogyakarta. Every evening, vendors line the pavements of Jalan Malioboro, one of the main roads in this Central Javanese city, with bamboo mats. Customers sit cross-legged on these mats to enjoy traditional *gudeg* (chicken cooked in jackfruit) and drink clear, sweet tea until the early hours of the morning.

WARUNG A *warung* is to Indonesians what the coffee-bar or the hamburger joint is to Americans. Customers may have a drink, order a quick meal cooked on the spot, nibble on snacks and exchange news or just while away some time. All a *warung* needs is a roof, a table-cum-counter to display jars of brightly-colored snacks and a bench for seating.

PADANG FOOD Eating Sumatran food is an experience. The table is laden high with a feast of anything from 10 to 25 varieties of food, all equally fiery. You just eat what you want and leave the rest.

A warung.

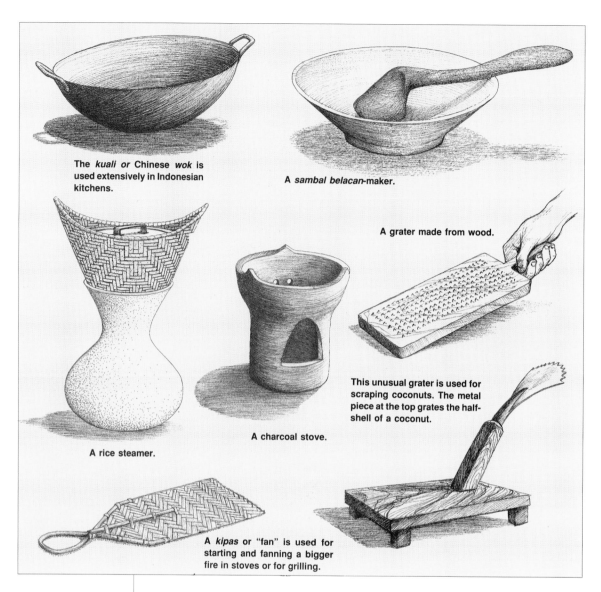

The *kuali or* Chinese *wok* is used extensively in Indonesian kitchens.

A *sambal belacan*-maker.

A grater made from wood.

A rice steamer.

A charcoal stove.

This unusual grater is used for scraping coconuts. The metal piece at the top grates the half-shell of a coconut.

A *kipas* or "fan" is used for starting and fanning a bigger fire in stoves or for grilling.

KITCHEN UTENSILS

Many of the kitchen utensils used are particular to Indonesia. Half a coconut shell attached to a split bamboo handle is used as a ladle to cook and dish out food. The simple wooden pestle and mortar is specially designed to efficiently grind the popular *sambal belacan* in just a few seconds.

Almost all kitchens will have a rice steamer, a special conical steamer made from strips of split bamboo which allows steam from the boiling water below to pass through the rice and cook it.

CONTAINERS

Food is not only cooked, but served and eaten, in a variety of disposable containers. One example is the ever-popular banana leaf, which is rolled, folded or cut to hold anything from steamed rice to barbecued fish. Bamboo joints are used to cook various meats and set yogurt, and coconut leaves are woven into traditional *ketupat* rice-cake holders.

Food wrapped in banana leaves is cooked in various ways—steamed, grilled, barbecued and even boiled.

	A	B	C	D	E
1	STRAITS OF MELAKA Banda Aceh Mt. Leuser ▲ Medan ● 2	THAILAND MALAYSIA SINGAPORE	SOUTH CHINA SEA	BRUNEI MALAYSIA KALIMANTAN 19	SULU SEA SULAWESI SEA Manado ● 22
2	3 ● Pekanbaru SUMATRA Padang ● 4 Jambi ● 5 6 7 ● Palembang Bengkulu ●	BATAM BANGKA Pontianak ● BELITUNG	Kapuas River 18 20 ● Palangkaraya Banjarmasin ●	Samarinda ● Mahakam River Barito River 21	Palu ● ▲ Mt. Poso 23 SULAWESI 25 24 Kendari ● MALUKU SEA
3	INDIAN OCEAN 8 ● Bandar Lampung 9 Jakarta ● 10 Bandung ● Semarang ● Mt. Slamet ▲ 11 Yogyakarta ● JAVA 13 12 N ↑ INDONESIA		JAVA SEA MADURA Surabaya ● 14 LOMBOK Denpasar ● SUMBAWA Mataram 15 SUMBA	Ujungpandang ● FLORES SEA 16 FLORES TIMOR Kupang ●	

			PROVINCES OF INDONESIA
Ambon F2	Java C3	Palembang B2	
	Jayapura G2	Palu D2	1 D. I. Aceh A1
Banda Aceh A1		Pekanbaru B2	2 North Sumatra A1
Bandar Lampung B3	Kalimantan D1	Pontianak C2	3 Riau A2
Bandung B3	Kapuas River C2		4 West Sumatra A2
Bangka B2	Kendari E2	Samarinda D2	5 Jambi B2
Banjarmasin C2	Kupang E3	Semarang C3	6 South Sumatra B2
Barito River C3		Seram F2	7 Bengkulu B2
Batam B2	Lombok D3	Sulawesi D2	8 Lampung B2
Belitung B2		Sumatra B2	9 D. K. I. Jakarta Raya B3
Buru E2	Madura C3	Sumba D3	10 West Java B3
	Mahakam River D2	Sumbawa D3	11 Central Java C3
Denpasar D3	Manado E2	Surabaya C3	12 D. I. Yogyakarta C3
Dili E3	Mataram D3		13 East Java C3
	Medan A1	Timor E3	
Flores D3	Mt. Leuser A1		
	Mt. Poso D2	Ujungpandang D3	
Halmahera E2	Mt. Slamet C3		
		Yogyakarta C3	
Jakarta B3	Palangkaraya C2		

PACIFIC OCEAN

HALMAHERA

Jayapura

26 SERAM
BURU
Ambon

PAPUA NEW GUINEA

27

BANDA SEA

ARAFURA SEA

17
Dili

TIMOR SEA

AUSTRALIA

	International Boundary
	Province Boundary
▲	Mountain
●	Capital
●	City
∿	River

14 Bali   D3
15 West Nusatenggara   D3
16 East Nusatenggara   E3
17 East Timor   E3
18 West Kalimantan   C2
19 East Kalimantan   D1
20 Central Kalimantan   C2
21 South Kalimantan   D2
22 North Sulawesi   E2
23 Central Sulawesi   E2
24 Southeast Sulawesi   E2
25 South Sulawesi   D2
26 Maluku   F2
27 Irian Jaya   G2

QUICK NOTES

LAND AREA
780,000 square miles

POPULATION
178 million

PROVINCES
D.I. Acheh, North Sumatra, West Sumatra, Riau, Jambi, Bengkulu, South Sumatra, Lampung, D.K.I. Jakarta Raya, West Java, Central Java, D.I. Yogyakarta, East Java, Bali, West Nusatenggara, East Nusatenggara, East Timor, Irian Jaya, Maluku, South Sulawesi, Southeast Sulawesi, Central Sulawesi, North Sulawesi, South Kalimantan, Central Kalimantan, West Kalimantan, East Kalimantan

MAJOR RIVERS
Musi, Batanghari, Indragiri and Kampar rivers in Sumatra; Bengawan Solo, Citarum and Brantas rivers in Java; Kapuas, Barito, Mahakam and Rejang rivers in Kalimantan; Memberamo and Digul rivers in Irian Jaya

MAJOR LAKES
Lakes Toba, Maninjau and Singkarak in Sumatra; Tempe, Towuti, Sidenreng, Poso, Limboto, Tondano and Matana in Sulawesi; and Mandai and Sentani in Irian Jaya

HIGHEST POINT
Puncak Jaya (16,500 feet)

NATIONAL LANGUAGE
Bahasa Indonesia

MAJOR RELIGIONS
Islam, Hinduism, Buddhism, Christianity

CURRENCY
Rupiah
(US$1 = 1790 rupiahs)

MAIN EXPORTS
Oil, gas, palm oil, rubber, tin

IMPORTANT ANNIVERSARIES
National Independence Day (August 17) celebrates the proclamation of independence in 1945; National Awakening Day (May 20) commemorates the establishment of the first national organization in 1908 which emphasized the need for unity to achieve national independence for the different Indonesian ethnic groups; Youths' Oath Day (October 28) marks the 1928 All-Indonesia Youth Congress which proclaimed the ideal of "one country, one nation and one language."

POLITICAL LEADERS
Mohammed Hatta—hero of independence movement and first Vice-President of Indonesia (1945–56)
Soeharto—army general who quashed the communist coup in 1965; second President of Indonesia (1968–)
Soekarno—charismatic leader who founded the political party PNI to gain independence from the Dutch; first President of Indonesia (1945–67)

GLOSSARY

adat   Customs, traditions and culture of a people.

animism   Belief that all natural objects (rocks, trees, etc.) possess souls.

bahasa   Language. Bahasa Indonesia is Indonesia's national language.

gamelan   A kind of Indonesian orchestra.

jamu   Traditional herbal remedy.

keris   Dagger with a wavy blade.

sambal   Spicy sauce made from ground chillies and served with rice.

stupa   Dome-shaped Buddhist shrine.

wayang   Drama using dance and music.

BIBLIOGRAPHY

Atmowiloto, A., *Indonesia from the Air*, Times Editions, Singapore 1986.
Dalton, Bill: *Indonesia Handbook*, Moon Publications, California, 1988.
Smith, Jr., Datus C., *The Land and People of Indonesia*, Lippincott, New York, 1983.
Zach, Paul and Edleson, Mary Jane, *Jakarta*, Times Travel Library, Times Editions, Singapore 1987.

INDEX

Picture Credits